Consumer
Insights 2.0

MARKETING BOOKS FROM PMP

The Kids Market: *Myths & Realities*

Marketing to American Latinos, Part I

Marketing to American Latinos, Part II

The Whole Enchilada: *Hispanic Marketing 101*

Beyond Bogedas: *Developing a Retail Relationship with Hispanic Customers*

The Mirrored Window: *Focus Groups from a Moderator's Point of View*

The Great Tween Buying Machine

Marketing Insights to Help Your Business Grow

Why People Buy Things They Don't Need

A Knight's Code of Business: *How to Achieve Character and Competence in the Corporate World*

India Business: *Finding Opportunities in this Big Emerging Market*

Moderating to the Max! *A Full-tilt Guide to Creative Focus Groups and Insightful Depth Interviews*

Marketing to Leading-Edge Baby Boomers

Clear Eye for Branding: *Straight Talk on Today's Most Powerful Business Concept*

Advertising to Baby Boomers

What's Black About It? : *Insights to Increase Your Share of a Changing African-American Market*

Marketing to the New Super Consumer: Mom & Kid

Hispanic Marketing Grows Up: *Exploring Perceptions and Facing Realities*

Religion in a Free Market: *Religious and Non-Religious Americans—Who, What, Why, and Where*

Beyond the Mission Statement: *Why Cause-Based Communications Leads to True Success*

Consumer Insights 2.0

How Smart Companies Apply Customer Knowledge to the Bottom Line

DONA VITALE

PARAMOUNT MARKET PUBLISHING, INC.

Paramount Market Publishing, Inc.
301 S. Geneva Street, Suite 109
Ithaca, NY 14850
www.paramountbooks.com
Telephone: 607-275-8100; 888-787-8100   Facsimile: 607-275-8101

Publisher: James Madden
Editorial Director: Doris Walsh

Cataloging in Publication Data available
ISBN-10: 0-9766973-8-6
ISBN-13: 978-0-9766973-8-1

Contents

Acknowledgments

CLIENTS, FRIENDS AND ASSOCIATES have been contributing to the ideas summarized in this book for more than twenty years. Thanks are due to every client who, even with reservations, said yes to a proposal for a weird new research project or a few experimental questions added on to a traditional study, just to see what we could find out. Without that support and trust, neither I nor my associates at Foote, Cone & Belding Advertising, nor my colleagues in the wider research community could have developed the non-traditional tools and techniques that are so important to the search for consumer insights. Thanks also to friends and colleagues in the Qualitative Research Consultants Association (QRCA) for sharing ideas and experiences that are an ongoing source of inspiration and creativity.

More specifically, I would like to thank, first of all, Peter McLennon, who first suggested I write this book twenty years ago. It's a better book than it would have been back then, but Peter's support and encouragement planted the idea and has kept it growing for two decades. I'd also like to thank my former Foote, Cone & Belding pals, Karen Randolph and Babs Zepaltas, for their creativity and insight over the years and for their support in the months that this book was in the works.

Special thanks also to Regina Lewis and her Consumer and Brand Insights Group at Dunkin' Brands, for so generously sharing their experiences and providing the background information for development of the Dunkin' Donuts case history. Of course, they also should be congratulated and recognized for having done the terrific insights work that gave me such a good case to document.

I would also like to thank the many people who have contributed to my Consumer Insights class at the University of Chicago Graham School, and by extension, to this book as well. Thanks to guest speakers Pat Swindle of Draft Worldwide, Barbara Weaver, another former FCB-er and Jan Lohs and Susan Sweet, fellow members of QRCA who shared their experience with the 2004 class, as well as Michelle Comer and Ginger Smithwick of Jockey International, who wowed them in 2005. Thanks in advance to Christopher Hogan of Kraft Foods, who has promised to speak in 2006, and to Rodrigo Placido, the former student who connected us. Richard Scovie, Coordinator of the Integrated Marketing Program at the Graham School also deserves recognition and thanks, for being open to the idea of a new course in Consumer Insights that was the initial basis for this book.

Last, thanks and appreciation to the friends who supported me through the writing process. Betty Welch Williams, Sharon Walker, Cynthia Capelli, Jean Templeton, and Harriet Russell are not in the business, but listened to my ideas anyway, offering encouragement when that's what I needed, and taking time off to play when I just needed a break. Thank you all for being my friends.

Part I

An Introduction to Consumer Insights

ONE

Why Consumer Insights Are More Important than Ever

IN 1992, Lisa Fortini-Campbell wrote *Hitting the Sweet Spot* and introduced the term "consumer insights" into the marketing vocabulary. To many of us in the advertising world, that little book was revolutionary. It documented a movement that had been going on for at least a decade among creative researchers, mostly in ad agencies, who were dedicated to the idea that insightful research, carefully done and thoughtfully analyzed, could lead to creative advertising that sells.

In 1992, Lisa talked about four trends that were making marketing tougher and making true insight into consumer needs and wants an essential ingredient for success. Since 1992, every one of these trends has accelerated. Today, we need consumer insights more than ever before.

When Lisa wrote of **new economic realities**, she was referring to the shift from an industrial to a service economy, declining real incomes, and loss of job security.

Fifteen years later, globalization has become the reality in every industry. Boeing no longer competes with McDonnell-Douglas and Lockheed for airplane contracts. Its new rival for worldwide airplane sales is the European company, Airbus. We buy drugs from pharmacies in Canada who obtain products manufactured in Ireland under U.S. patents. The strawberries on our breakfast cereal might be from Mexico or Argentina. A phone call to our local bank's customer service department might be answered in India. Even when consumers want to "buy USA," they find few products on the shelves that fit the description anymore.

Along with increased global commerce has come a continuing high level of immigration and **an increasingly multi-cultural society** at home. The high school in my multi-ethnic Chicago neighborhood includes students from sixty-five countries and twenty states, but new-comers to America are no longer restricted to dense inner-city neighborhoods. Between 1990 and 2000, the foreign-born populations of states like Arkansas and Kentucky more than doubled. Schools in small Iowa towns struggle with how to educate the Spanish-speaking children of Mexican meat-packers. The trend even led the U.S. Census Bureau to coin a new word, micropolitan, to describe a rural town that looks more and more like its culturally diverse big-city cousins, but on a smaller scale.

These pressures and others have contributed to **increased polarization on political and social issues.** The 2004 election introduced the idea of Red States and Blue States, representing opposing views of the world. Post-election, we've learned it's not that simple. Conflicts in values don't just occur among people in easily identified geographical areas—and may sometimes be found trying to co-exist within the same consumer's complex take on the world.

New technology also figured heavily in the marketplace in 1992, when Lisa talked about the rise of new communications channels such as cable television, direct marketing, toll-free-number telephone service, desktop publishing, and an explosion of advertising in media such as shopping carts and school TV. Fifteen years later, add increasingly easy Internet shopping, bloggers, instant messaging and texting over cell-phones that have become so common that a modern-day Superman would have a hard time finding a good phone booth where he could change clothes. Even newer are "reality" TV and opportunities for product placement limited only by the marketer's imagination and the media's craving for new infusions of cash.

These factors combine to create **more competition** for the consumer's time, money, and energy. In 1992, retailers were already beginning to exert the new power of information teased from point of sale scanners and the increasing presence of national chains like Wal-Mart. Today, "big box" stores are ubiquitous, and large chains have become even larger. To compete with Wal-Mart, Sears and Kmart have merged, Target has made itself into an "upscale" discount store, and Federated continues to buy up local department stores to create national chains that can compete on the same turf. As leverage against retailer control, manufacturers are working harder to build their own brands, solidify customer relationships, and shave costs to stand up against the brutal competition created by easily-accessed Internet price comparisons.

Partly in response to these trends, and partly as a result of demographic inevitability, **changing consumers** are a continuing force in the marketplace. In 1992, increased product choice and greater availability of information fueled a drive toward one-to-one marketing. In the intervening years, "mass customization" has become a way of marketing life, as increasingly Internet-savvy consumers design their own new cars or kitchens on-line, or compare prices from hundreds of vendors in seconds by using websites such as Froogle or Yahoo Shopping.

Baby Boomers are older than in 1992, but still dominate many markets. The influence of aging Boomers has shifted focus in financial services from credit cards and college savings plans to retirement planning and long-term care insurance. In apparel, we are seeing the rise of "middle-aged fashion" brought to us by retailers like Chico's and Eileen Fisher. Even Hollywood has started producing movies of interest to the adult audience, not just teenagers.

GenXers have grown up. Dismissed as slackers searching for their identities in 1992, this group fueled the technology boom of the 1990s and learned valuable lessons of entrepreneurship and independence that make them tougher customers than their parents ever were.

And of course, the up-and-coming GenY Millennials are fighting our wars, making music and poetry, and growing up comfortable with both new technologies and new fears that the rest of us once knew only from science fiction. As a group, they are as large as the Baby Boom generation, and marketing to them will require approaches unlike anything that has been done in the past.

In response to these external pressures, today's leading marketers are rethinking the way they collect, analyze, and use all forms of marketplace intelligence. Organizations that have traditionally limited their marketing research departments to an objective-information-gathering role removed from actual decision-making are now demanding more from their information specialists. They are redefining goals and retraining researchers to seek broader, deeper, and more creative views of their markets and to find fresh insights into the needs, wants, hopes and fears of the target consumer. New **consumer insights specialists** use a wide range of disciplines and methods, building on objective facts to infuse the entire organization with a consumer-based perspective that drives all aspects of the business.

In this book, I want to share what I've learned in more than twenty years of seeking consumer insights for marketers in more than thirty industries, ranging from food and household products to computer technology, politics, and tourism. First, we'll take a more detailed look at how consumer insights is different from traditional marketing research, and what it takes for the insights approach to be successful. We'll look closely at how one major company has integrated consumer insights into every aspect of its operations to transform itself for the 21st century. Then we'll review the latest knowledge about what makes consumers think, behave, and talk the way they do. I'll share tools I've used to develop meaningful consumer insights for my clients, and to sum up, we'll take a look at how individuals can develop their own ability to find insights, and how corporations can build and support an insights-driven culture.

TWO

What Does "Consumer Insights" Mean and Where Did It Come From?

A Brief History

IN THE EARLY 1970s when I first went to work for Foote, Cone & Belding Advertising in Chicago, research professionals in advertising agencies were beginning to grapple with an increase in the size and influence of client-side marketing research departments. Before this time, only a few of the largest marketers maintained a marketing research staff, while smaller companies relied heavily on their agency partners to provide the information and insight needed to develop marketing and advertising campaigns. By the 1970s, that had changed. Clients had established their own marketing and marketing research functions, and they began to wonder what a research person at the ad agency could contribute that the dozen or more researchers just down the hall could not. At FCB, we began to wonder too.

Meanwhile, in London, ad agencies faced with the same question were beginning to adopt an innovation first proposed in 1965 by British advertising executive Stanley Pollitt. Pollitt recognized that the ever-increasing supply of marketing information was overwhelming the capacity of account managers, media planners, and creative people to process it and apply it to strategic decisions. He believed that researchers had the most ready access to information about the consumer and the skills most appropriate for analyzing and using it. Yet, most of the time, researchers were relegated to the agency back room, expected to crunch numbers and supply facts but then give up their place at the table when decision-making began. To use information more effectively, Pollitt proposed making the research specialist the consumer's representative in the agency, charged with knowing what the consumer thinks, feels, and wants, and with applying that knowledge to the development of advertising strategy, putting the researchers on an equal footing with the other members of the account team.

In 1968 Pollitt was able to implement his idea when he became a partner in a new agency, Boase, Massimi Pollitt. In the same year, with much the same goal, J. Walter Thompson in London formed a department called "account planning," headed by researcher Stephen King. While the two agencies had slightly different approaches to "planning," as the new discipline came to be called, their early successes drew attention, and within a few years, many London agencies were beginning to establish account planning departments of their own.

Back in Chicago, we began to notice that FCB's London office, newly reorganized to include account planning, was winning recognition as the most creative location in the company's worldwide network. What interested us most was that London was not only doing creative advertising, but that the account planners were developing creative new approaches to research unlike any of the traditional methods we were using. They were incorporating ideas from a wide range of academic disciplines, and they frequently used several complementary approaches to address the same issue. They spent relatively little time on advertising evaluation, concentrating instead on the beginning of the process, doing work that would contribute to the development of relevant but unexpected advertising strategies.

A few years later, American agencies began experimenting with the account planning model. (FCB was late in the game, without a formal planning function until the nineties, long after I had moved on to my own qualitative research practice.) As mentioned earlier, in 1992, Lisa Fortini-Campbell, one of the early planners in Chicago, wrote *Hitting the Sweet Spot*, subtitled *How Consumer Insights Can Inspire Better Marketing and Advertising*. By the mid-nineties, account planning became accepted practice in advertising agencies around the world.

In the meantime, clients were talking about "voice of the consumer" research and came to the realization that "consumer insights" can inspire better decision-making in parts of the organization that may not play a direct role in advertising and marketing. Long term planning, new product development, customer relations, corporate communications, channel management, and other areas of operations are all more successful when decisions are informed by a fundamental understanding of the end consumer.

Beginning in the late 1990s, consumer marketers for large companies began incorporating some of the new ideas of account planning into their own operations. At first, change was signaled by the addition of a reference to strategic planning in the title of the marketing research department. Eventually, the new approach was reflected in entirely new titles for employees who were charged with gathering, interpreting, and applying information, with disseminating relevant knowledge throughout the organization, and with representing the perspective of the consumer at the decision-making table. Today, an information specialist may be called Director of Consumer Knowledge Development, Director of Consumerology, Manager of Consumer and Market Knowledge, Director of Market Intelligence, VP of Strategy/Insights, or any number of other similar terms. The most common titles, used at Kraft Foods, General Mills, Pepsico, Unilever, The Gap, Target, Motorola, McDonald's, Citicorp, and dozens of other major consumer products companies include consumer insights or some variation of that term.

Undoubtedly, in some organizations, the title change was only cosmetic, with very little change in the departments carrying the new name. In most, however, the change of title is the outward sign of a complete revolution—a new way of operating, a new way of using information, and a new way of applying information to decision-making.

What Is the Consumer-Insights Approach?

So, how is insights-driven research different from traditional marketing research as we used to know it? One practitioner describes it as "getting inside the head of the consumer and seeing things from her point of view." Others emphasize the need to go beyond facts, to use consumer knowledge as a foundation for decision-making. All agree insights-driven research needs to delve deeper and work harder to inform and inspire consumer-focused marketing.

In many ways, that's not so very different from the way marketing research has always been done by the best people in the best companies. It's the kind of research that doesn't just stop at describing *what is,* but pushes to understand *why.* It's the research done by forward thinkers who put more value on studies designed to guide the future than on documenting the past. It's the research that seeps into every crevice of the organization—so that everyone who touches the consumer relationship, from the CEO to front-line customer service staff, know the person to whom the company is marketing, and how that customer thinks and feels about the company's product and its place in her life.

It is very different from research done to validate or support decisions that have already been made without the benefit of much consumer knowledge. It's different from technique-driven research that stops with generation of a number or score, with little illumination of the dynamics behind that finding. It's not the kind of research that's done for one specific purpose, presented once to a limited audience, and then filed away to gather dust. And, it's different from research that stops with presentation of the facts and leaves others to determine how to apply the learning to real business problems.

Companies typically embrace consumer insights with the goal of making marketing information and research more productive and relevant within the organization. An apparel manufacturer realized that research would be more valuable if it could go beyond analysis of data detailing *retrospective* information on the sale of individual items and brands to *prospective* guidance as to what might sell better in the future. A provider of consumer services felt a need to "humanize" the research function, using information to bring the customer to life for everyone within the organization. A major food company saw that more effectively leveraging its consumer knowledge would provide an important competitive advantage in its industry.

The common thrust of these examples is a drive toward forward action, toward application of information to on-going business problems, and to integration of ideas about the consumer into all aspects of decision-making. The emphasis on action paired with integration into all aspects of the organization represents the major differences between consumer insights and traditional marketing research.

In most organizations, marketing research is viewed as a staff function, a service department existing to serve the needs of decision-makers in brand management, marketing and sales, new product development, corporate communications, and any other department in need of marketplace information. Researchers in these traditional settings conduct studies to address questions or issues posed by others, and talk about the research initiators as their "internal clients."

In contrast, the most effective consumer insights specialists talk about their "team members" or "colleagues" when referring to co-workers in other job functions. In an insights-driven setting, researchers have more responsibility for initiating research. They are charged with identifying and acquiring whatever information the company needs to run its business and to prepare individual decision-makers to make strategic choices. They are more involved in the interpretation and application of research findings to business issues, and are expected to be strong advocates for the conclusions and implications they draw from their investigations.

In most dictionaries, "insight" is defined as the ability or power to see and understand clearly the inner nature of things. Having or gaining insight is the act of understanding or *seeing intuitively* the inner nature of an object or situation. The definition stresses the action of getting below the surface, to the "inner nature" of what is being investigated, an essential objective of consumer insights research.

We also think of insight as a flash of immediate understanding that comes when someone recognizes relationships or makes new associations to help solve a problem. Insight is the "aha!" idea that may come unexpectedly all at once, but it is usually based on long study and a deep understanding of the subject under consideration. Albert Einstein may have come up with $E=mc^2$ in a flash of inspiration, but before that moment of revelation could happen, he spent years studying everything there was to know about mathematics and physics.

A person looking for insight is most successful when focused on the problem, looking for the underlying principles or concepts that might provide illumination, rather than adhering to a particular process or way of thinking. In consumer insights, that means finding or creating methods of investigation that are most appropriate to the question or issue at hand, rather than relying on a limited repertoire of established research techniques. Some British researchers describe the approach as "bricolage," drawn from a French word that means "to tinker around and build from whatever materials may be available." A "bricoleur"—a researcher who engages in bricolage—creates things from scratch, resourcefully collecting information from a variety of sources, and putting it together in an innovative way.

To get a better understanding of the consumer's point of view, consumer insights calls for looking at problems from a variety of angles and perspectives. Some practitioners emphasize taking a 360-degree look at the consumer, that is, examining all aspects of the consumer's life, not just the situation or occasion in which a particular product comes into use. Others emphasize triangulation, addressing the same objective with two or more methods of investigation, perhaps by supplementing a survey on shopping habits with in-store observation, or conducting both focus groups and in-home interviews to more fully understand usage and attitudes.

Consumer insights research incorporates a wider range of methods and disciplines than typical marketing research, which tends to place a heavy emphasis on survey research and psychology-based concepts and methods. Consumer insights specialists also do plenty of surveys, and draw on psychological principles and analytical methods in much of what they do, but they also incorporate a wide range of other disciplines into their work.

Sociology and social psychology provide valuable insights into how people form groups and behave in groups, what factors influence individual and group behavior, how people develop the attitudes and beliefs they hold, and how attitudes and beliefs are influenced by outside forces such as marketing.

Cultural anthropology looks at the ways people interact and express themselves within their culture and how a culture reflects the values of the people in it. Ethnography, the technique cultural anthropologists use to study cultures, has become an over-used (and frequently misused) buzzword in consumer insights research, but the principles behind this methodology make an important contribution to the toolkit we use to mine for meaningful understanding.

The relatively new field of **neuropsychology,** research on how the brain works as an organism or mechanism, has produced findings that have important implications for how we think about how people think, feel, and process their sensory experiences.

Data mining and database analysis also contribute insights. Just crunching numbers isn't enough. When creative analysts tease out the implication of results discovered by mining masses of data on the characteristics and behavior of individual consumers, new perspectives can emerge.

Semiotics and linguistics give us ways to look at how individuals and cultures express ideas, and how to read the signs and symbols that surround us every day. **Futurists** help us look at what lies ahead, making planning more realistic in our rapidly changing world. These and other academic disciplines provide the multi-faceted prism through which consumer insights are revealed.

Consumer insights also require a solid foundation of **business principle and practice.**

Esoteric academic methodologies can lead to fascinating learning, but this learning has little value to the organization unless it can be applied to concrete business problems. Insight means nothing if it ignores the bottom line or does not take into account the likely cost and potential return of the activities it guides. Insight is useless if it suggests actions that countradict the organization's mission and long-term objectives, or cannot be executed within the organizational structure, regulatory framework, or market environment that exists or can be developed. The study of consumers is a business activity, never just an academic exercise.

Consumer-Insights Techniques Are Varied

As might be expected from the wide range of disciplines used in consumer insights, the approach also makes use of a wide range of data-gathering methods. Some practitioners emphasize qualitative interviewing, others lean toward observation and ethnography. Still others favor quantitative analysis of survey data and transactional databases. The best, however, are true *bricoleurs,* incorporating any or all these approaches to their investigations as called for by the immediate problem at hand.

Techniques that provide decision-makers with direct consumer contact are an important aspect of consumer insights. Well-educated, well-paid business people working in corporate settings have lives that are very removed from the everyday experiences of many of their target consumers. Because of this distance, they may have a distorted or idealized vision of who those consumers really are, what they need and how they live. In fact, it's not unusual for observers attending focus groups made up of people recruited from their own definitions of the target market to be surprised by how "real" consumers look, talk, and dress, or even how they use the product in question.

To provide consumer contact, insights-oriented companies may encourage on-site field work by having decision-makers go along on in-home interviews, retail "shop-alongs," and other opportunities for learning about the consumer in a natural consumption or purchase situation. Others may go further to facilitate interaction. One major food company sets up consumer immersion days, where members of a brand team invite consumers to the company's test kitchens for a few hours of informal cooking and conversation. A manufacturer of audio-visual equipment has its professionals attend weddings as assistants to the videographers hired to record the occasion. In both companies, participants come away with a new understanding and deeper appreciation for the consumers who make up their target markets.

In the search for insights, practitioners seek information from a variety of subjects. In traditional marketing research, interviews are almost always conducted with "typical" target audience members, because the desire is to learn about the most common behaviors and attitudes and build marketing programs to fit them. Insight, however, sometimes comes from examination of the atypical—the extreme user, the non-user, the leading-edge adopter, the role model, or the expert. Consumer insights also places more emphasis than traditional research on information gleaned from intermediaries in the purchase and consumption process. Dealers and distributors, recommenders and influencers, installers or repair persons, sales staff, or service providers are frequent subjects of research.

A triangulated study of a food product, for example, might supplement interviews with or observation of direct consumers by adding talks with restaurant chefs or wait staff, magazine food editors, nutritionists, school lunchroom ladies, or grocery buyers. A study on local transportation services will certainly include individual commuters, but might also gather information from bus drivers, parking lot attendants, or the passenger service representatives who give travel routing assistance over the telephone. Each additional group included in the analysis adds another perspective and another opportunity for getting below the surface of the question.

Technological change has made new tools for data collection and analysis available and consumer insights *bricoleurs* have been among the first to adopt and refine these methods. Pencil-and-paper or phone-and-computer surveys have been supplemented, or in some cases, replaced, by surveys, focus groups and extended bulletin board chats done over the Internet. Interviews that ask respondents to remember how they felt or behaved during a purchase or usage situation can be replaced by "in the moment" data collection by consumers who keep audio or video diaries or respond to pager messages and record their thoughts and actions on handheld PDAs. Interviews and field observations can be documented with easy-to-use digital cameras and video recorders that help bring marketplace experience back to the home office. Sophisticated data-mining algorithms uncover unexpected relationships that would otherwise remain hidden in the powerful but ever-enlarging databases generated by daily business transactions.

Communication Is as Important as Insight

By definition, insight is an intuitive understanding of a problem or situation. The implication is that insight originates within an individual person, one who develops an insightful understanding of a situation and then must communicate the idea to others before the organization can take action. That makes persuasive communication of insights at least as important as the process of generating them. It does no good for one member of the team to have a brilliant flash of understanding, if he or she is unable to share that perspective with others in a clear and convincing way.

Because open communication is so essential to success, most insights-driven companies have (or soon develop) a culture that encourages information sharing and collaboration. The approach is rarely successful in organizations where hard and fast structural boundaries inhibit the free exchange of ideas or where turf-protection is the accepted means of operating. Effective use of information and insights can drive decisions only when the atmosphere of the corporation encourages, or at least permits, cooperation, risk taking, creative thinking and experimentation.

Consumer-insights practitioners spend time thinking about how sto communicate their ideas to others in ways that go beyond simple presentation of thick report books or endless presentation decks. In some insights-driven companies, results of a major insights investigation might be presented to other team members in a seminar or workshop format that starts with the information exchange and moves quickly to a group effort to apply results to forward planning. In other organizations, insights specialists spend a great deal of time in informal conversations with their colleagues, sharing their knowledge when and where it can most usefully be applied. Sometimes, they act as facilitators of creative brainstorming sessions to help teams build on the information they have gathered. Often, they are charged with assessment of strategic plans and marketing programs to determine whether they are truly insight-based and executed, or to determine how better insight might lead to greater success. All of these approaches help energize thinking within the organization and help put the consumer at the center of everyone's thinking.

THREE

The Art of Insight: What It Takes and How to Get It

ALMOST ANY INDIVIDUAL or team can occasionally come up with a brilliant insight about the consumer or marketplace, but an insight-driven organization doesn't depend on serendipity, waiting for these magic moments to occur. When a company focuses on consumer insights, the goal is to develop a process for using information that consistently produces unique and relevant understanding of target audiences, brands, and competitive environments.

The consumer-insights approach is a blend of art and science, grounded in established principles and techniques, yet highly dependent on the creativity and intuition of the individuals who apply them. The most successful practitioners of consumer insights have personal characteristics that make them especially good at finding and sharing insights combined with the skills and competencies they need to acquire solid information on which to base their ideas. The most successful insights-driven companies are those that develop an organizational structure and corporate culture where such practitioners can be most effective. The combination of the right people, with the right skills, in the right organizational environment creates a situation where the insights approach can thrive.

The Consumer-Insights Personality

Most people can learn the basic research and business skills they need to find and apply insights, but not everyone has the personality to make consumer insights a wise career choice. People with experience in account planning and consumer insights generally agree that the most successful practitioners in the field have most or all of ten specific personal characteristics.

1. **Curiosity** is fundamental. Successful consumer-insights practitioners are inherently interested in lots of different things. As children, they not only asked "why is the sky blue?" but took the trouble to go to the library or dig through their science textbook to find the answer. They have a strong need to know about the world around them. As adults, they have retained the habit of wondering why, in business as well as in daily life. They are people who are tuned in to their immediate environment and to what's happening in the wider culture. They are usually well read on a variety of topics. They keep up with the latest books, movies, music, and TV shows, just to see what everyone is talking about. They are probably well-traveled, or at least interested in traveling to new environments and experiencing other cultures.

2. They are **open-minded** in their thinking. They are always willing to discover a new piece of information, or to consider an issue from another point of view. They may have a well-developed belief system, and may live their life by an established set of guiding principles, but they are never dogmatic or doctrinaire. Whether considering a business theory, a social issue, a philosophical approach, or a religious tenet, they remain intellectually open to the possibility of a new idea or new piece of information that can alter their thinking.

3. **Creativity** is a habit. Consumer insights require original thinking, and successful practitioners display this ability in many aspects of their lives. They are divergent thinkers who can easily come up with many different ideas or questions about a topic, and whose tendency is to avoid immediate acceptance of the "right answer" according to conventional wisdom. They have vivid imaginations, and are not afraid to use imagination to come up with new expla-

nations of common phenomena or new uses for everyday items. They enjoy and value the arts, and are likely to engage in some form of personal artistic expression such as making art or music, writing poetry, or dressing with a particular individual flair.

4. They approach work and life with **energy and enthusiasm.** They work hard and get excited about the work they do. They enjoy learning, thrive on discovery, and love being able to share their insights with others. They are enthusiastic about the brands and categories they market, and show respect for the products they work on and the consumers who buy them.

5. They are **organized but flexible.** They carefully manage their tasks, time and intellectual output without being rigid or resistant to change. They organize their work by setting goals and deadlines, making plans, and executing them well. They organize their thinking by structuring theories and models to explain the facts of a market or situation, and are able to articulate a coherent story or develop a clear picture from seemingly unrelated bits of data.

6. They have a **preference for multi-tasking.** They are not only *able* to juggle many different tasks, projects, and ideas, but they actually *enjoy* doing so. Not only do they keep many project balls in the air and running smoothly, they can consider many different ideas simultaneously, remembering, relating, and making new connections all the time.

7. They are **confident and self-assured.** A good consumer-insights specialist must be an independent thinker. The other members of their marketing team depend on them to bring innovative and original thoughts to the table. To be effective, they must have the confidence to put forth their ideas and the self-assurance to discuss and defend them without feeling threatened or defensive. They should feel energized and stimulated by questions and debate, and be willing to accept challenges, building and refining their ideas as others provide input and reaction.

8. They have a **"can-do" attitude.** An optimistic belief that there are

insights to be found is an essential quality in someone whose career success depends on coming up with fresh ideas day after day. Persistence is important as well. Successful insights practitioners keep looking, even when no great revelations seem to be emerging. They step away and try a different approach. They are not easily deterred from the quest for understanding.

9. They are able and **willing to experiment.** To find new insights, they are willing to try new approaches, maneuvering through uncharted territory if necessary to get the information they need. They enjoy exploring and experimenting with creative new approaches to information gathering, and they are willing to take calculated risks to try out new techniques or put forth new ideas.

10. They must be **team players** who are comfortable with a supporting role and do not always have to be the star. Much of the success of the insights approach depends on the ability of one team member to convince the rest of the group of the soundness of his or her point of view. It takes tact, patience, and sometimes even a willingness to back off and let others take credit for a good idea. A person who can't or won't let a teammate shine will not be successful in consumer insights.

The Skills and Competencies Used in Consumer Insights

Along with the right personality, consumer insights specialists also need a specific set of skills to do their jobs. These competencies can be developed through a combination of academic study and on-the-job experience in a variety of fields. Because formalized positions in consumer insights are relatively new, most practitioners have experience in other functional fields, as well as varied academic backgrounds. But, whatever their individual backgrounds, most share a core set of competencies.

1. Most importantly, consumer insights specialists must have a thorough grounding in **marketing research methods and practices.** They must be especially good at defining information needs and designing research studies to address them. They should be "quick

studies," who know how to use existing internal and external resources to delve into a new issue and get up to speed in a hurry. They should also know how to get formal research studies done. Sometimes, insights specialists conduct their own qualitative research or design and implement their own surveys, especially those done on the internet. Sometimes, they engage the services of outside research vendors, consultants, and academic experts to conduct studies. In either case, their own knowledge of the principles of marketing research are an essential component of high-quality work.

2. Along with a grounding in marketing research, consumer-insights specialists must be **fluent readers of the meaning of numbers.** Advanced mathematical or statistical skills are not particularly useful in consumer insights, but the ability to manipulate and analyze numeric data from a variety of sources is essential. Equally important, successful consumer insights practitioners are those who are best able to "translate" numbers into words and visual diagrams that quickly convey the meaning behind the statistical data.

3. Consumer insights also calls for strong **strategic thinking and problem-solving** skills. Insights specialists must be able to see "the big picture" and the long view of any situation. They must be skilled at identifying the heart of an issue or problem, and they must be able to chart a clear path to their goals, taking into account internal opportunities and challenges as well as environmental factors or social and cultural constraints.

4. They must be **excellent communicators**, in writing, in formal presentations, and in everyday one-to-one conversation. Clear, concise, and persuasive writing and presentation skills are essential. Insights specialists must also be able to discuss and debate, and think on their feet to apply their findings to specific business issues.

5. **Project management** is an important part of insights, and practitioners must be able to keep many individual projects on track, on time and on budget. With insights at the center of an organiza-

tion's information gathering and analysis activities, the job calls for coordination with co-workers and monitoring of outside resources to anticipate needs and deliver timely information.

Some of these skills can be developed in most business management or marketing positions, which is one reason consumer insights draws people from many different backgrounds. More specialized research and analysis capabilities usually come from a combination of academic or on-the-job training. Since consumer insights is a new field, few college or graduate school courses address the topic, so practitioners and potential newcomers to the field must be ever alert to new learning opportunities.

Insights-Friendly Corporate Culture

Organizations that benefit the most from consumer insights have incorporated a focus on the consumer into everything they do. Top executives believe in the importance of understanding what the consumer wants. CEOs cite consumer insight as a key element of corporate strategy and talk about their commitment to consumers, comfortably and frequently, with employees, investors, and anyone else who will listen. They understand that consumer-driven, insights-based marketing can provide long-term growth that will keep their companies strong for years to come.

Employees in these companies respect and value the consumer. Their goals are to provide the products and services consumers want and need, by building brands that stand for something consumers value. They want to know their consumers better, and they know that every genuine insight helps them be more successful, whatever their specific job function.

The consumer insights group occupies a clearly defined position in the organization and is accessible to the whole organization, not just to marketing. It works with any department or function that needs better information about the marketplace or external environment, bringing consumers into focus for everyone. Insights specialists are involved early in the strategic planning process, charged with responsibility for generating basic consumer and brand information that becomes a foundation for long-term planning for all business activity. Sharing information in a form that is meaningful to each functional group within the company is an important responsibility, and in fulfilling this role, the insights group may also facilitate better interaction among departments with little previous contact.

Of course, the consumer insights group also takes responsibility for fulfilling the day-to-day information needs of its marketing colleagues, and may spend much of its time conducting routine marketing research to shed light on everyday marketing decisions. However, even as they fill this need within the organization, insights specialists strive to consider each finding within the broader context of their total body of knowledge, drawing on everything they know or believe about the consumer as they tease out the implications of individual tactical studies.

When a company focuses on the consumer as a primary source of guidance and inspiration, the commitment seems to foster collaboration and cooperation. Debate and discussion over the interpretation and meaning of information allows for the free exchange of ideas before decisions are made. Across departments, plans and programs are based on the same fundamental understanding of the market, so coordination of activities becomes easier and diverse units of the business communicate in a more unified voice. Brand building becomes a system-wide goal, and brands become stronger as a result.

Some people also believe that the consumer-insights approach improves focus and removes, or at least reduces, the influence of corporate politics. Armed with appropriate consumer-based knowledge, individuals and departments become more interested in building their strategies on market-oriented realities, rather than being led astray by alluring but inappropriate ideas. Confidence in the company's strengths and assets grows, and decision-makers can say no to ideas with little potential or with too much risk attached, regardless of who within the company is championing them.

Achieving this kind of corporate culture is not easy. It doesn't happen overnight. It certainly doesn't happen just because someone changes the title of a department or individual position to include the words consumer and insights. It takes understanding, commitment and a lot of work. But, for many organizations, it also has become an essential step on the path to greater success in the modern marketplace.

In the next chapter, we take a look at one company that has successfully incorporated the consumer-insights model.

FOUR

Using Insights for Transformation: Taking Dunkin' Donuts from Good to Great in a Changing Marketplace Environment

STARBUCKS. KRISPY KREME. Low-carb diets. Trans-fat controversies. New breakfast competitors. New bakery options. Premium coffee everywhere you look, even at McDonald's.

Life in the coffee-and-baked goods business hasn't been easy in recent years. Yet Boston-based Dunkin' Donuts is experiencing record sales growth, withstanding every challenge and serving more than 800 million cups of coffee every year, plus enough doughnuts, bagels, muffins, breakfast sandwiches and iced drinks to generate more than $3 billion in annual sales.

What's behind the Dunkin' Donuts success story? One major factor has been the work of the Consumer and Brand Insights Group, the Dunkin' Brands research team. The development of the insights group at Dunkin' Brands reflects a trend occurring throughout corporate America, as "marketing" research expands beyond marketing and customer-conscious corporate leaders recognize the value they gain from insisting that real insights guide decision-making. The story of how the Consumer and Brand Insights Group has helped transform Dunkin' Donuts is a powerful example of how consumer insights can contribute to corporate success.

A Bit of History

In 2003, when new CEO Jon Luther took over leadership of Allied Domecq Quick Serve Restaurants, he found an established marketing research department already guiding the introduction of espresso-based coffee drinks into the company's Dunkin' Donuts outlets. From that foundation, Luther and his new management team built the Consumer and Brand Insights Group (CBIG) that, in 2005, he called "the engine that drives the business" at renamed and reinvented Dunkin' Brands.

Although probably best known as the workplace of Fred the Baker and his mantra, "It's time to make the doughnuts," the chain's coffee sales have long exceeded revenue from other items. In its New England home, outlets are everywhere, and picking up coffee at Dunkin' Donuts is a morning ritual. Elsewhere, the brand is well-known and well-liked for its coffee, operating in thirty-six states and twenty-nine countries worldwide. Yet, in 2000, CBIG researchers could see that the national expansion of Starbucks had changed the ready-to-drink coffee market. Category tracking showed strong growth in cups-per-day, and a sharp rise in afternoon consumption. The increases were concentrated in espresso-based drinks, a category Starbucks virtually owned and in which Dunkin' had no entry. Firmly established as a provider of good coffee brewed as an accompaniment to freshly-made breakfast baked goods, Dunkin' Donuts was in danger of being left behind.

To assess the situation, Dunkin' researchers conducted a major hot coffee usage and attitude study that looked beyond the quick serve category and the chain's traditional breakfast day-part. The study showed that Dunkin' customers were also frequenting other types of coffee establishments, and provided a good look at the identity and attitudes of those who were buying espresso-based coffee most often. These insights into the newly challenging competitive environment launched a spirited debate as to whether to add espresso products to the menu.

It wasn't an easy decision. It was clear that espresso introduced as a "me-too" response to Starbucks was unlikely to succeed. The Starbucks welcoming ambience of couches and fireplaces and leisurely lounging was a mismatch with the bright, utilitarian style of Dunkin' Donuts outlets and busy down-to-earth lifestyles of its patrons. There was a real fear that complex, foreign-sounding drinks like Mocha Cappuccino and Vanilla Soy Latte might alienate core Dunkin' customers. Another complication was that espresso drinks can be slow and difficult to make. Store-to-store quality would be hard to guarantee. Even worse, a "grande, half-caf, low-fat, double-shot latte" could bring drive-through service to a halt while morning regulars, anxious for their usual coffee and breakfast sandwich, waited and fumed. The risks of espresso loomed large, even as the debate within the company heated up.

Not willing to let the issue slide, the researchers analyzed market data to assess the opportunity cost of not moving forward. The results were compelling. Tracking studies showed continuing category growth, with strong penetration among upper-income groups, especially women aged 25 to 49, a market segment Dunkin' was unwilling to relinquish without a fight. Equally important, most espresso drinks, like other coffee, were purchased on-the-go and in the morning, making espresso a direct threat to the chain's core business, and almost impossible to ignore.

The challenge was to figure out how espresso would work at Dunkin' Donuts.

A critical insight was that, in spite of the changing marketplace and the heated-up competitive environment, the brand was strong. Dunkin' Donuts was part of a morning ritual for its loyal regulars, but at the same time, customers gave the brand permission to innovate. In fact, given all the recent interest in coffee, customers looked forward to a more accessible, more affordable line of espresso-based products from their favorite chain.

Working closely with the company's innovation team, Dunkin' researchers helped incorporate the consumer's perspective into every aspect of the introduction. Operational decisions such as equipment choice and crew training took the consumer's speed of service expectations into account. Extensive sensory testing made sure the products themselves were appealing. Positioning and communications research identified cues to enhance the espresso experience. Advertising research found the right message, the indulgence and revival espresso drinkers crave with convenience that other coffee places can't deliver.)

In 2003, "Espresso for Everyone" was introduced in time to capture a solid spot in a category that has continued to show steep growth ever since. Initial advertising positioned the new line directly opposite Starbucks and its "third place" clones. In one commercial, a harried mother with a baby in the back seat is struggling to get into a too-small parking space in front of the local coffee place, when she spots passers-by carrying cups of Dunkin' Latte. A voice-over says "Discover a latte that's delicious, indulgent and a whole lot more convenient. Dunkin' Donuts' incredible new latte. It's rich, it's creamy, and it's so much easier." The frustrated coffee-seeker spies a Dunkin' outlet down the block, pulls up to the drive-through, and in just a moment, drives away with a revitalizing drink.

The Starbucks mystique was challenged. The democratization of espresso was underway. A good research department did its job, and contributed to a successful new product introduction. But that was only the beginning.

Transforming Research to Insights

When Jon Luther and his new management team accepted the charge to reinvent Dunkin' Donuts, it was already the largest "coffee and . . ." chain worldwide. But about half of all U.S. outlets were in New England, where the chain dominates the ready-to-drink coffee business. Expansion of Dunkin' Donuts into a truly nationwide brand is one of the key elements of the corporate strategy, along with revitalization of the Baskin-Robbins franchise and further development of Togo's, a small West Coast sandwich business.

To achieve these goals, Luther undertook a corporate reorganization to streamline decision-making. The goal was to place more emphasis on brand-building while also energizing franchisees and inspiring them to ever-higher performance. Key members of the leadership team included brand leaders responsible for marketing, operations, and local development, a Menu and Concept group charged with innovation and operational oversight, and a Strategy group with responsibility for planning future growth in all aspects of the business.

As part of the reorganization, the marketing research function was repositioned as a corporate information resource. Reporting to the Corporate Strategy officer, not the marketing department, the renamed Consumer and Brand Insights Group soon became known throughout the company by its acronym, CBIG, which reflects the "big picture" strategic orientation the group assumed. Today, CBIG works closely with every decision center in the organization, getting involved in all aspects of operations, from brand marketing and new concept development to restaurant excellence and franchisee relations.

When CBIG was created, the first task was to find a dynamic leader to head the department. A nationwide search led to the hiring of Regina Lewis, a seasoned marketing researcher with a strong blend of corporate, entrepreneurial, and academic experience. Lewis joined the company in December 2003, and immediately began to reshape the existing research department to fit its expanded mission.

When she took over CBIG, Lewis found a capable pool of talent in need of structural support and leadership. The department had no budget of its own. The only research that could be done was what brand marketers requested or could be persuaded to sponsor, because they controlled all budgets. The result was that attention and resources were devoted to tactical marketing questions, but there was little opportunity to address the big strategic questions that would ultimately drive the corporate reinvention.

"My team members were great," Lewis says, "but they were not appreciated. They had very little opportunity to decide what to research—to pose the questions that needed to be answered. At best, they could shape methodology, but mostly they were executing projects that someone else thought were needed, rather than identifying what information would contribute to the company's success and then going out and getting it. That was one of the first things I knew had to be changed."

Enlisting the cooperation of another new arrival, John Gilbert, Vice

President of Marketing for Dunkin' Donuts, Lewis negotiated a budgeting change that became the means of shaping CBIG's focus and operating strategy. "John was a true ally, not an opponent," she says. "He was also new, and we saw eye to eye on what needed to be done. His support was, and continues to be, tremendously helpful."

Instead of funding research projects through direct charges to individual brands or programs, CBIG now manages a budget that includes line items for the kind of research typically requested by marketing and other departments, but also funds studies with broader company-wide applications that are initiated by Lewis and her group. Under this system, CBIG does the concept tests, sensory tests and positioning studies that other team members need to guide their work, but manages and prioritizes so that the most effort remains focused on research that addresses the most important strategic issues.

"My job is to help people, but you have to have the power to say no," Lewis says. "When someone requests information, sometimes we do a new study, and sometimes we are able to provide what they need through existing research. Before we made the change, no one was looking at all the research that was getting done. This system helps us manage our information resources much more effectively," she adds.

Once the new budgeting system was in place, Lewis turned her attention to staff development and training. The new, more proactive role for the department called for a different style than under the previous system. "I needed to encourage people to be initiators, not order-takers," Lewis says. "We need fantastic researchers who can back off from the day-to-day and look at the critical questions, then take the initiative for getting them answered."

Creativity and a willingness to experiment are highly valued within CBIG. Research projects must be methodologically sound, but once that requirement is met, staffers are encouraged to try non-traditional approaches to get a fresh look at the consumer. "Nobody ever gets in trouble for trying to do the right things or trying to experiment," Lewis says. "I want my people to have the freedom to do great work, and that means having the freedom to fail once in a while."

Lewis also expects staffers to have great communication and presentation skills, and to be persuasive in their interactions with colleagues throughout the company. To develop these skills, she spends a large chunk of her time in one-to-one interaction with subordinates, modeling the cooperative work style she finds most effective. On the job training is supplemented by outside workshops on subjects such as dealing with conflict or getting things done through persuasion and negotiation. Collaboration with colleagues throughout the organization is the CBIG mantra.

With budget in place and staff development underway, CBIG was in the ideal position to energize and guide the brand-building effort. Innovative, strategic research projects have helped Dunkin' Donuts understand the essence of its brand and the fundamental structure of its competitive market environment. Insights research has helped shape a long string of successful new product introductions, and helped build a completely new Dunkin' Donuts concept store that provides the model for expansion into new markets. Each piece of work adds to what has come before, and Dunkin's increase in consumer understanding has been matched by growth in sales and profitability.

Understanding the Essence of the Brand

Soon after Lewis arrived on the scene, CBIG launched a multi-faceted study of the meaning of the Dunkin' Donuts brand. Working from the belief that consumers buy brands that help them define themselves, understanding how the Dunkin' Donuts brand works was the essential driver of every element in the strategic plan.

The Dunkin' Donuts brand platform builds on the idea of "Rituals that Revive." Research showed that stopping for coffee in the morning gives consumers a sense of control, preparing them to deal with the demands of the day while providing a transition from home to work. Cutting through the morning fog, a stop at Dunkin' is something to look forward to, that provides both a boost and a last mellow moment before the day begins in earnest. Afternoon customers experience a slightly different revival, as picking up something from Dunkin' provides a chance to refuel as well as a cozy treat, a reward that smooths the way through the rest of the day.

This understanding of the coffee-drinking ritual is an important insight into consumer motivations, but in an increasingly competitive environment, does not lay down a unique foundation for brand-building. CBIG knew that its primary task was to understand what Dunkin' Donuts can provide to its customers that other coffee establishments cannot.

Recalling the thinking behind the next major piece of research, Lewis says, "We innately all know Dunkin' Donuts is loved for its down-to-earth style and is a brand for 'real people,' but this had never been articulated or put on paper to help build our brand strategy." So, CBIG set out to explore how "realness" works for Dunkin' Donuts.

Working with Dr. Bob Deutsch, an anthropologist known for helping advertisers probe the deeper meanings behind their brands, CBIG initiated a brand research project which would articulate why people love Dunkin' Donuts and why "real people" go there.

To provide an intensified consumer experience that would create the sharpest contrast between two key brands, the project included a deprivation study, in which regular Dunkin' Donuts customers in Chicago, Boston, Phoenix, and Charlotte were asked to forego visits to the chain for a week, directing their business to Starbucks instead. An equal number of Starbucks loyalists in each city were asked to do the same, substituting Dunkin' Donuts for their trips to Starbucks. After the deprivation period, the research participants were interviewed one-on-one to collect their in-depth reactions to the experience.

Results of this study reinforced hints found in earlier research that Dunkin' Donuts and Starbucks rarely compete head-to-head for the same customers. Instead, each brand appeals to its own "tribe,"and members of which gravitate toward the coffee provider that most closely matches their own personalities and lifestyles.

From an anthropological point of view, the Dunkin' Donuts and Starbucks tribes exhibit classic signs of differentiation. They hold different beliefs about themselves and the world. They exaggerate the differences between their own "in" group and the other tribe. They even speak different languages. At Dunkin' Donuts, the smallest serving is a small, while at Starbucks, the same size cup is called tall. Diet-conscious Dunkin' customers ask for coffee with skim milk. At Starbucks, the low-cal order is a non-fat latte.

When each set of respondents was asked to give impressions of the other store, the differences were striking.

Loyal Dunkin' Donuts customers rejected virtually every aspect of the Starbucks experience. They said the coffee is too strong and too expensive. According to the Dunkin' tribe, "real people don't have $6 for a cup of coffee." They described Starbucks customers as ambitious, career-driven yuppies who go to a place designed as a relaxing hang-out but insist on using their cell-phones, laptops, and Blackberries even while placing their orders. Starbucks people spend too much time on themselves, and are not at all family oriented. They are hard to please and pretentious, going to great lengths to make even a simple coffee purchase a complicated expression of their individuality.

Starbucks customers were equally disdainful of Dunkin' Donuts. Going to Dunkin' Donuts was like going to a blue collar truck stop, they said, where the coffee is too weak and the rest of the menu is limited to a few bland, uninteresting choices. The stores themselves are bright, cold, sterile, and loud, designed to get customers in and out in a hurry, without having to provide a relaxing atmosphere, personalized service or an opportunity to express individual preferences. To the Starbucks tribe, Dunkin' Donuts was nothing more than another fast food joint.

The deprivation study developed a clear picture of the differences in the customer bases of the two brands, but more research was needed to see how the brand's characteristics matched with consumers' feelings about themselves and about authenticity or "realness." To get at this question, CBIG conducted focus groups with people not included in the deprivation study, in the same four markets. In each city, one group of loyalists to each chain talked about "realness" in terms of themselves, the brands they use, and other aspects of their lives.

That research provided clear direction for making Dunkin' Donuts "real" to its customers and potential customers.

Efficiency is a key. "Real" Dunkin' Donuts people are proud to have things to do and places to go. They have no time for idle conversation and don't want to waste time waiting for their morning coffee order. They are often hurried and usually feel scrutinized—time is short and has to be accounted for. They seem to always be "on the go," on the way to the next place they have to be, but take some pride in not having time to relax. They appreciate that Dunkin' Donuts serves up the efficiency they need to manage their busy lives.

Dunkin' Donuts people see themselves as "regular, average" people who want "a regular cup of coffee for a regular guy." They are down-to-earth and don't worry about appearance or fitting in. They also don't need the "status boost" that can come from keeping people out. They like that Dunkin' Donuts is for everyone, not an exclusive place where only the cognoscenti are comfortable, and they reject the Starbucks mystique. For them, "Coffee is not an existential moment."

Dunkin' people "sweat for their money" doing "real" things. They are the construction workers, police officers, social workers, and teachers who keep society running smoothly with their consistent pragmatism and simple, straightforward values. They like routine and stick with what they know because it works. They appreciate the simple pleasures in life. Just getting a seat on the train to work can make the whole day go better.

From this research, CBIG identified "the regular guy" as the core of the Dunkin' Donuts brand persona. The study provided insight into how the brand helps customers celebrate the ordinary and everyday events of life, providing them with internal gratification rather than external affirmation. Dunkin' Donuts asks "real people" to join its community of kindred spirits, inviting you, the consumer, to spend time with a brand as comfortable with itself as you are with you.

To remain true to this core identity, CBIG recommended that advertising embrace the Dunkin' Donuts customer, celebrating the Regular Guy, regular values, and regular coffee. The advertising team was urged to stay away from aspiration casting and to stick with the "real" Dunkin' Donuts personality in every piece of marketing communication.

"It has become clear to me that our customer is our best voice," says marketing vice president John Gilbert.

The result? A new ad campaign introduced in New England late in 2005 invited Dunkin' Donuts customers to submit real stories about the "great lengths" they have gone to for their favorite cup of coffee. One commercial to emerge from these real life testimonials features a woman who introduces herself and says, "this really happened to me." She then tells us about the time she got a flat tire on the way to work one morning, but "after thinking about it, I decided my need for Dunkin' Donuts coffee outweighed my need for a tow truck." The visual shows her riding on the flat, right up to the Dunkin' drive-through, before dealing with her tire problem. As she drives off with her morning cup, she continues, "In the end, my medium regular with extra sugar ended up costing a few hundred bucks, but it was worth it."

The "real people" approach, refined and evolved, continues in New England, and will be the vehicle for opening new markets as the national expansion progresses.

The Dynamics of the Young Coffee-Drinker Market

Also in 2004, CBIG conducted on-line interviews with a nationally representative sample of more than 6,000 16-to-54-year-old past-week buyers of beverages for immediate consumption. Zeroing in on specific beverage consumption occasions, the study asked for details of purchase and consumption that allowed CBIG to segment both customer types and occasions, looking for untapped markets for existing products as well as new product and new market segment opportunities.

That research generated information that led to interest in young adult coffee drinkers, who became the subject of another innovative CBIG undertaking.

The overall objective of the Young Adult study was to understand the thoughts, feelings and motivations of 16-to-22-year-olds when they consider drinking, or actually drink, either hot or iced coffee. The initial research showed consumption patterns that generated a long list of additional questions, including identification of the varying needs associated with coffee, and the nature of the coffee-drinking experience. Researchers wondered whether coffee is seen by young adults as an individual or a social experience, and how hot coffee, flavored coffee, and iced coffee differ in the emotional gratifications they provide. In addition to the emotional background, CBIG needed to answer practical questions such as what set of stores this segment considers when each type of coffee comes to mind, what other beverages might be considered competition for specific drinking occasions, how often the originally planned coffee purchase or destination changes in reality, and what influences the ultimate choice of drink and outlet. Results would guide promotion of current products to young adults as well as shape development of new products designed to address any unmet needs the research might uncover.

A traditional approach to such questions would have involved doing a few focus groups to "get a feel" for the target group, followed by a large-sample survey asking about the details of the occasions and motivations surrounding purchase of different types of coffee beverages. But the information that a survey would generate was already available from the earlier beverage consumption study. CBIG needed a more creative approach to generate meaningful new insights.

The result was an innovative study in which 16-to-22-year-old coffee drinkers were recruited to carry around hand-held digital recorders, making entries in an audio diary each time they bought coffee or thought about doing so. Analyzing the hundreds of entries made over the course of the study, CBIG was able to gain insight into the many roles coffee beverages fill in the lives of young adults.

Among other opportunities, the study identified the need for "chugable energy," as described in this actual diary entry:

> "It's 10:40 in the morning, on Saturday, and I'm on my way home. I had decided I would stop at Dunkin' Donuts. Instead, I'm going to a diner. . . . I got an Iced Mocha Latte. I decided I was a little thirsty and I didn't want just some hot coffee that I had to sip. I really needed a pick-me-up so I decided to get something fun. I don't think I've ever had one of these before. . . . It's pretty good. It's pretty sweet, but it's good. I would consider this a treat every once in a while, though. I wouldn't have this all the time."

Insight from entries like these led to development of Turbo Ice, a new espresso-charged iced coffee promoted with tongue-in-cheek tortoise-and-hare advertising in which the slacker tortoise buys a Turbo Ice and gains a last-minute surge of energy that leads him to victory in a race against the hare. Customizable with any of nine flavor options, Turbo Ice builds on the "coolness" factor of coffee for young adults and takes it to a whole new level.

Keeping a Steady Finger on the Pulse of the Consumer

With its major 2004 strategic research initiatives underway, the next CBIG challenge was to develop a mechanism for obtaining quick consumer feedback on a wide range of issues. Traditionally, most day-to-day tactical research questions have been addressed with random-sample telephone surveys conducted as needed. However, in the last decade or so, response to telephone surveys has declined precipitously. Answering machines, call screening, abandonment of land-lines in favor of mobile telephones, the absence of incentives for participation, antagonism to telemarketing, and concerns about privacy have all contributed to consumer unwillingness to participate. Today, on average, telephone surveys produce completed interviews with only about 7 percent of the random sample contacted. The result is less reliable data that costs too much and takes too long to obtain. CBIG needed a more creative solution.

After considering alternatives, the company decided to invest in development of a proprietary on-line panel of Dunkin' Donuts customers. Working with a research firm with experience in panel creation and drawing on the Marketing and Field Marketing teams for assistance, CBIG recruited customers to participate in its VIP Advisory Panel. Built by promising participants tangible incentives as well as the opportunity to have a meaningful voice within the company, the panel quickly became a ready mechanism for quick feedback on a wide range of issues. In just a few months in the summer of 2004, for example, randomly selected members of the VIP panel provided input on more than a dozen projects, ranging from short surveys on favorite summer drinks, drive-through usage, and preferences in coffee lids, to the creation of the optimal breakfast sandwich, a study that laid the groundwork for development of the Supreme Omelet sandwich introduced in early 2006.

Outside the VIP Panel, CBIG also conducts on-line studies to guide and refine every aspect of the company's brand-building effort. Regular brand and advertising tracking, on-going product development and positioning research and intense analysis of new market opportunities represent a large chunk of CBIG's day-to-day activities. The result has been a string of successful new and revamped product introductions, from Turbo Ice and the Tropicana Coolatta, to a complete redesign of the Dunkin' Donuts packaged coffee bag to better reflect the brand personality.

Refining Every Aspect of the Retail Concept

CBIG's next big challenge was to drive innovation in all aspects of the Dunkin' Donuts retail concept in preparation for the chain's accelerated expansion into new markets nationwide. The goal was to optimize the retail concept, retaining the brand's many strengths while revitalizing the franchise and moving to a new level of excellence.

The project was a collaborative effort that extended into every aspect of the company. CBIG background briefings identified cultural trends that provided insight into the mindset of the post 9/11, post-Katrina consumer. Brainstorming sessions with participants from every brand team and department identified a broad range of possibilities to be tested.

A crucial need was to create an approach that could organize and sort through the plethora of new ideas. Building the optimal new concept store would require detailed examination of individual characteristics to understand how all possible combinations of options would drive both store usage and profitability.

For test purposes, the research team developed detailed descriptions of possible scenarios, taking into account a long list of variables, including:

- Store type, exterior and interior appearance and mood
- Brand and slogan variations
- Uniforms
- Hours of operation
- Seating area and table service options
- Counter service, speed, and ordering options
- Drive-through issues including number of lanes, speed, and express service options.

As part of each scenario, the team included estimates of the incremental cost to franchisees or corporate operations associated with every option, so results of the consumer feedback could be evaluated in the context of a profitability analysis

Once the final list of items to be tested was complete, CBIG commissioned a study of 1,005 in-person interviews conducted nationally among quick-serve restaurant patrons. In each interview, respondents answered questions about their last purchases of food or beverages during four day-parts from early morning to evening. Then they were presented with one of the concept scenarios, including a menu, and asked how likely they would have been to go to this restaurant instead, had it been available on that particular occasion. Additional questions recorded what the respondent would have ordered from the proposed menu, allowing for an assessment of the revenue that each scenario would generate.

Based on the results of this survey, CBIG scored each individual operational detail based on its ability to attract visits and its ability to generate revenue. Then, based on the individual scores, the team "re-assembled" all possible restaurant and menu combinations to forecast visits and spending. Overlaying the cost of each option, the forecasts allowed for calculation of the resulting profitability of various alternatives.

A new Dunkin' Donuts concept store opened in late 2005 in Pawtucket, Rhode Island. It retains the familiar pink and orange color scheme, the basic, comfortable table seating and overall simplicity that consumers value. However, it also steps up fresh food options, features Grab 'N Go options, and improves on speed and efficiency to meet the demands of on-the-go consumers. As Regina Lewis describes it, "We wrapped all these elements—all the things consumers have requested of us, and more—in an atmosphere that is, undeniably, at its soul, Dunkin' Donuts. Not the Corner Bakery, not Panera Bread, but Dunkin' Donuts. We have been true to ourselves."

"Customers love it," she adds, and provides numbers to back up the assertion. Seventy-three percent of consumers say that, based on the new store, Dunkin' Donuts is "way ahead" of competition, 89 percent would recommend the new store to a friend, 94 percent say the new bakery case is "much better" than competitors, and 83 percent give the new store higher marks on freshness.

"How have we succeeded?" Lewis asks, and then answers her own question. "By asking consumers. And then asking them again, a different way. And then asking them yet again, a different way still."

And then, of course, turning the answers she gets into insights that inspire transformation.

Part II

The Foundations of Insight:
Understanding Consumers From Every Angle

FIVE

How Consumers Behave

ALBERT EINSTEIN is said to have claimed, "It is the theory that decides what we can observe." When searching for consumer insights, it is useful to start with a theory to provide structure and meaning to our research and observation.

Since the emergence of marketing as a business discipline in the mid-twentieth century, both practitioners and academics have searched for theoretical models that can be used to explain consumer behavior in the marketplace.

Why do customers buy your service? What attracts the target audience to your product category? Where are consumers most likely to learn about your offering? How do potential buyers process the information they receive from advertising and other marketing communications? When is the most opportune time to influence their purchase decisions?

To provide answers to these questions, some theorists have developed complex explanations, diagramming every aspect of the consumer's information-seeking and decision-making process with dozens of boxes, arrows, and dotted lines, ultimately leading to a satisfactory purchase. Others have drawn from disciplines such as psychology, anthropology, or economics to explain how people buy. Some avoid formal explanations, but rely on a mix of past experience and personal intuition to represent their individual views of how and why the marketplace operates.

The one sure thing we can learn from this abundance of models is that there is no single explanation for consumer behavior. But any

and all of these approaches can provide insight into consumer decision-making, and it is usually a good idea to build a structured model
of consumer behavior when investigating an unfamiliar product category or trying to come up with a fresh look at an established market.
The trick is understanding enough about the category and the consumer to identify which model is most applicable, and understanding
the model well enough to apply its basic principles to the situation
you are studying.

Most models deal with more than one aspect of the decision-making process. Almost all try to identify how potential buyers find out
about a product or service they need. Some go more deeply into how
people develop or recognize a need that the product or category can
fulfill. Others relate more to what factors influence the choice to buy,
or not to buy, a particular product or an individual brand within a
specified product category. A few try to explain the dynamics of a
marketplace, that is, who will and won't buy, when purchases will
take place, what causes repeat purchases or creates customer satisfaction. Many of the earliest models were developed to explain how
advertising works, but most can be applied to all aspects of marketing communication, as well as to non-commercial efforts at persuasion, such as political campaigns.

Let's review some of the most widely used and commonly accepted
models.

Economic Utility Model

The earliest buyer-behavior models were developed by economists,
who typically looked at consumer behavior as a completely rational
calculation that takes into account the costs and benefits of any potential purchase. According to classical economic theory going back to
Adam Smith, buyers choose goods that maximize utility, that is, those
that provide the most benefit or satisfaction for the cost required to
obtain them.

This is the theory that says, all things being equal, the lowest
priced product will sell the most. The theory predicts that lowering a

product's price will increase sales. Or, adding more utility, in the form of extra features or benefits, to a product otherwise identical to that of the competition will cause consumers to prefer it. In its purest form, the theory says each additional unit of utility adds exactly the same value, while modifications of the theory take into account the possibility of a non-linear relationship between variables that might make some features or benefits more valuable than others.

FIGURE 5.1

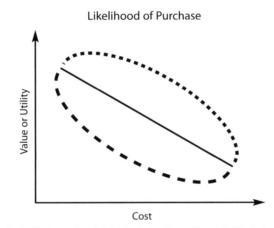

Source: Philip Kotler, "Behavioral Models for Analyzing Buyers," *Journal of Marketing,* October 1965

In 21st century marketing, there are many situations in which the economic utility model continues to operate. In true commodity markets, product is completely undifferentiated and price is the only basis for choosing one supplier over another. The internet has also fostered a return to utility-based purchasing in many categories. With only a few mouse-clicks, potential buyers can directly compare the features and benefits of many competing brands and models, or get a quick survey of the selling price for a specific product on a wide array of retail sites.

In other categories, marketers behave as though economic utility is the controlling factor, even when it tells only half the story. Most airlines set prices as though this model perfectly explains air travel behavior, providing low fares to leisure travelers who may not have a preference for one flight, or even one travel date, over another, while charging more to business travelers who place higher value on issues such as schedules and flexibility, and can be counted on to pay more for a ticket on the flight they need. Whole departments work full-time changing prices several times a day, while others within the same organization spend their careers trying to negate the operation of this model by creating more utility for their brand, establishing frequent flyer programs, offering more leg room, or building brand image by painting planes or putting flight attendants in newer, more glamorous uniforms.

When working in a category where the utility model might be operating, it's important to understand how the consumer defines the variables of cost and utility. Brand image can create intangible utility for some consumers that may be difficult to take into account. Costs can include more than the monetary price of a given product, encompassing factors such as the ease of making the purchase, the difficulty of maintaining the product, or the expense of keeping a supply on hand. Value can be affected by the perceived advantages and disadvantages of add-on features or extra services. Small differences in price may not be important enough to influence choice, or might not even be noticed in a fragmented or rapidly changing marketplace.

Pavlovian Learning Theory

We all remember learning about Pavlov's dogs that were taught to salivate at the sound of a bell, expecting food even when they did not get it. Some marketers use the same technique of conditioned response to promote their products, through repetitive advertising, trial-generating promotions, and constant reinforcement of a simple message designed to create immediate product demand. In the heyday of broadcast media, most marketers seemed to subscribe to this theory, no matter what the product. Large advertising budgets and far-reaching media made it possible to pound home a product message with repetition, until even small children knew that "R-O-L-A-I-D-S spells relief."

The Pavlovian model is most applicable to situations in which a single, simple message or image can trigger the desired response, or when most choices deliver the same basic benefit. Many food and drink categories fit this description, and it is no accident when a billboard featuring a giant-sized Whopper appears just a few blocks away from a Burger King restaurant. It worked on Pavlov's dogs, and it works on us.

Conditioned response can have a strong negative impact on a category if marketers reinforce consumer behavior that is counterproductive in the long run. A retailer who runs one sale or special promotion after another may gain in the short term, but over time, this strategy conditions customers to buy only when a price reduction is in effect. Packaged goods marketers, who eliminate brand-building activities like advertising and rely on their promotional activities to move product off the shelf, are conditioning their customers as well. In categories where this strategy is common, consumers lose track of what they like about individual brands and start buying "whatever is on sale" because something always is. When this happens in your category, look closely at consumer needs and desires to find a way to break the conditioned habit and instill new energy into the marketplace.

Social-Psychological Model

At the end of the nineteenth century, Thorsten Veblen wrote *The Theory of the Leisure Class*, introducing the idea that behavior is influenced both by the expectations of an individual's peers and his or her aspirations to become part of a more prestigious reference group. This insight has been a driving force in marketing for almost a hundred years, and shows no sign of losing validity any time soon.

In Veblen's day, the aspirational group was the leisure class, wealthy individuals whose conspicuous consumption served as a model of "the good life," which the lower classes tried to emulate as closely as possible with substantially fewer financial resources.

Today, some consumers may aspire to the lifestyles of the rich and famous, while others seek to emulate hip-hop artists, star athletes, or idealized supermoms with great jobs, perfect children, and husbands who share the housework.

In any category where products act as status symbols or convey "badge" value, it is essential to understand everything you can about the reference group your target consumers look up to, and how your product helps consumers reach their aspirational goals. To gain this insight, look for the symbols and emotions linked to your product, which are likely to be much more important to consumers than product features or benefits.

Freudian Psychoanalytic Model

In the 1950s, Freudian psychoanalysis was in vogue, and motivational researchers like Ernest Dichter explained consumer behavior by positing that middle-aged men buy red convertibles as a substitute for taking mistresses, or that woman bake cakes as an act of creation reminiscent of giving birth. A backlash begun by publication in 1957 of Vance Packard's book, *The Hidden Persuaders*, reduced the direct influence of these Freudian ideas in marketing, and yet we still accept the importance of understanding subconscious motivations and decoding the symbolic significance that everyday objects and images may hold for consumers.

In searching for consumer insight, the legacy of Freud is a reminder to look for ways to access thoughts, feelings, and behaviors that may lie below the surface of the consumer's consciousness. These hidden nuggets may stem from the Freudian unconscious, but may also be habitual actions of which the consumer is no longer aware, or cultural assumptions that are so deeply ingrained that their influence on decision-making is obscured. Emotions, prejudices, sensory perceptions, and the influence of archetypes, myths, and dreams are other aspects of the consumer's mind where deeper exploration is likely to yield valuable new understanding.

Hierarchy of Effects: The Linear Approach

One of the first models created by marketers to explain how advertising works was published in 1961 by Robert J. Lavidge, a leading marketing researcher of the time, and Gary A. Steiner, a professor at the University of Chicago. This model, widely used in advertising and marketing textbooks in the sixties and seventies, said that advertising must move people through a series of steps in a logical order that goes from total ignorance of the product's existence to, ultimately, selection and purchase. It's called the Hierarchy of Effects model because the authors believed that each step had to happen in a specific order, and that potential purchasers had to move up each notch on the hierarchy without skipping any stages.

Followers of this model believe that consumers must first be provided with factual knowledge about a product, and that this knowledge will affect their emotions by creating liking and eventual preference for the brand in question. Reinforcement of preference at point of purchase will create conviction of the brand's desirability, leading to purchase. In this model, the earliest stages deal with presentation of *rational* facts and features, the middle of the hierarchy depends on an *emotional* reaction, and the final step leads to the *action* of making a purchase.

FIGURE 5.2

Hierarchy of Effects

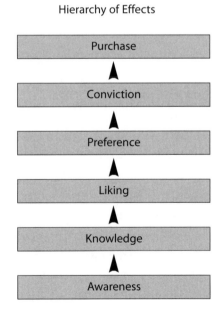

Source: Robert J. Lavidge, and Gary A. Steiner, "A Model for Predictive Measurements of Advertising Effectiveness," *Journal of Marketing,* October 1961.

While this process doesn't apply to every product category, it is relevant to many marketing situations, and the steps in the hierarchy are worthy of consideration in almost every case.

New product introductions, especially in high-tech or otherwise complicated categories, often must start at the very bottom of the hierarchy and inform consumers that an innovation has occurred, teaching them enough about the features and benefits of the new technology to create desire or liking before a purchase happens. It's hard to imagine a typical on-the-go business executive hearing the name Blackberry and instantly wanting to buy, but once the right potential users learn that this little device can keep them connected to e-mail and the Internet anywhere and anytime, they are likely to feel a strong emotional desire to own one, and purchase is only a matter of time.

Involvement Theory and the Learn-Feel-Do Circle

Although the Hierarchy of Effects model gained wide acceptance in marketing and advertising, it was not long before even its advocates began to see that passage through the hierarchy is not always linear. The idea that marketing messages can have an effect on consumers even when they are barely noticed and not remembered was first put forth by Herbert E. Krugman, a prominent researcher who differentiated between "high involvement" and "low involvement" processing of advertising messages in the mid-1960s.

When consumers are highly involved, Krugman said, they actively process the logical arguments made in advertising, passing through the three stages of the Hierarchy of Effects. They first learn facts, which lead to formation of favorable attitudes, which in turn lead to preference and purchase. However, in many cases, Krugman pointed out, consumers simply do not put forth this amount of effort, and may, in fact, barely perceive that they are being exposed to a marketing message at all. Nonetheless, these exposures, over time, can have a powerful effect on behaviors, beliefs, self-image, and core values, all without conscious examination of the content of their messages.

Depending on the category or situation, consumers may skip from awareness to an emotional response, or make an instantaneous impulse purchase, without processing factual knowledge or making a comparison with competitive brands or ideal standards. This insight led to development of the Learn-Feel-Do model, which says purchasing behavior can be stimulated in a variety of ways, sometimes through laying out a logical and persuasive message, sometimes by tapping into a meaningful emotion, and sometimes by prompting action without waiting for thought or feeling to take effect. This model draws on the idea that different parts of the brain are used to process different types of information. The part of the brain commonly referred to as the left brain, the seat of logic and rationality, is where _learning_ takes place, and where information about product features, benefits, and effects are stored. The right brain is where we process _visual imagery, sensation, or emotion_, reacting to whole pictures, sounds, smells, and symbols without breaking them into individual bits of data, or sometimes, without being consciously aware of the stimulus to which we are reacting. These methods of information processing lead us to the "blink" moments described by Malcolm Gladwell in his recent book of that name. We react before we consciously think, without going through the linear stages of earlier models.

Instant "right-brain" processing explains why Target can run ads featuring a red and white bull's-eye graphic and no brand name, or why one look at the famous Swoosh reminds us to step into our Nikes and "Just Do It." After a compelling image or brand is established, simply providing consumers with the familiar symbol brings up a host of related associations. Cognitive "left-brain" thinking, on the other hand, takes over when we read a whole page of product features in a direct-mail piece on the latest version of our favorite software package, carefully assessing the value of each improvement as we logically decide whether to upgrade or not.

Recognition that consumers may process marketing information in a variety of ways was an important step away from the one-model-fits-all thinking characteristic of earlier work in this field, but simply drawing the Learn-Feel-Do Circle did not explain when each mode of thinking was dominant, nor when it was most appropriate to direct marketing messages toward either the right or left brain functions. To answer these questions, marketers turned to the concept of "involvement" for guidance.

FIGURE 5.3

The Learn-Feel-Do Circle

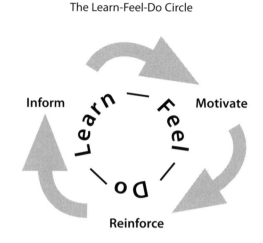

Krugman defined "involvement" as the degree to which a consumer finds "bridging concepts" in a marketing message. A bridging concept, he said, is a connection, or personal reference, between a message or other stimulus and the consumer's own life. A message with many bridging concepts that the consumer consciously recognizes will generate a high degree of personal involvement as the consumer processes the ideas being presented. Once the message has been processed, the consumer is either persuaded or rejects what's being offered. Only a few exposures are needed for a high-involvement message to have its maximum effect. When the consumer is exposed to a message without bridging connections, he or she receives it more passively and more repetitions are needed for the message to generate an attitude change or a shift in behavior.

Elaborating on Krugman's ideas, other theorists added detail to the definition of high involvement. Personal relevance, the novelty or complexity of the message, and its relationship to a consumer's deeply-held values, self-image, or desired self-presentation have come to be recognized as factors that influence our involvement in a particular product, purchase, or message. High involvement situations are those to which the consumer commits energy and focus, while low-involvement is characterized by the consumer's passivity and inclination to devote little effort to the task at hand.

The FCB Grid

Working with the ideas put forth by Krugman and other involvement-theory advocates, Richard Vaughn, then a research director at Foote, Cone & Belding Advertising, created an advertising planning model that came to be known as the FCB Grid. Looking for an explanation of *how* and *why* advertising works, Vaughn combined involvement theory with the concept of brain-specialization and plotted the relationship between these ideas on a two-dimensional grid. In this model, Vaughn theorized that category-specific purchase decisions and other aspects of consumer behavior can be analyzed and mapped based on the degree of involvement they generate and the balance they strike between left-brain rational thinking and right-brain emotional response. According to Vaughn, decisions that fall in different quadrants of the grid have different decision-drivers and should be treated differently in advertising and marketing.

High-involvement products that generate left-brain thinking activity call for an informative approach, with lots of specific information presented in environments where consumers have time to assimilate the message and reflect on it. Magazines, websites, and direct-mail pieces are all good settings for products in this quadrant.

High-involvement *feeling* products, on the other hand, call for approaches that convey brand imagery and lifestyle values the consumer can emulate and to which he can relate. Aspirational products fit in this quadrant, best presented through visual imagery, role models, and appeals to the consumer's core values.

FIGURE 5.4

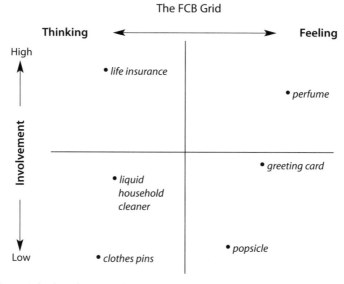

The FCB Grid

Source: Richard Vaughn, "How Advertising Works: A Planning Model," *Journal of Advertising Research,* October, 1980.

Low-involvement thinking products are those the consumer may initially choose based on perceived differences in features and benefits, but continue to purchase largely through habit. According to this model, new products may start out in the high-involvement quadrant but eventually slip in involvement as they become more familiar. In these situations, marketing efforts need to continually reinforce the consumer's purchase habit, and from time-to-time increase involvement to attract new users to the category or take business from competitors. Many household products fit solidly into this quadrant, supported by reminder advertising, in-store promotions and the occasional introduction of "new and improved" versions to shake up otherwise stable product categories.

Low-involvement products that rely primarily on right-brain processing depend more on sensory feelings than on emotional response. This quadrant is the home of "treats" that provide sensory satisfaction—beer, cigarettes, simple toys, candy, fresh fruit, and similar low-cost, low-risk products best promoted with simple messages and lots of pictures.

Conversion Theory

A related approach designed to explain consumer brand choice within a category has been drawn from sociological research on religious conversion. In this model, consumers can be arrayed on a continuum based on their degree of commitment to a brand, from the most loyal, through the "convertible," to the opposite end of the spectrum—those most loyal to competing brands.

This model distinguishes between the *behavior* known as loyalty—defined in marketing as repeated purchase of the same brand—and the *psychological attachment* known as commitment. Conversion theory says that loyalty may be the result of habit, convenience, or the lack of available alternatives, factors that have little to do with product performance or customer satisfaction. Commitment, on the other hand, comes when consumers have a strong attachment to the product, whether they purchase it every time or not. Commitment comes when involvement is high and may cause the consumer to overlook minor defects in his or her choice.

By determining which of a brand's purchasers are truly committed, which are merely loyal, and which may have these feelings for more than one brand, a marketer can address different strategies to each group, making marketing efforts more productive.

Diffusion of Innovation

Another theory that relates more to the dynamics of the marketplace than to the behavior of individual consumers is the Diffusion of Innovation Theory. This model explains how new ideas, practices and products are introduced and gain acceptance within a culture. Its basic premise is that diffusion, or adoption of something new, is a process that takes place gradually, in five stages that tend to follow a typical curve.

The five categories are: innovators or true originators of a new practice, early adopters, early majority, late majority, and laggards. Each group adopts the innovation in turn, until the idea has spread throughout the society.

FIGURE 4.5

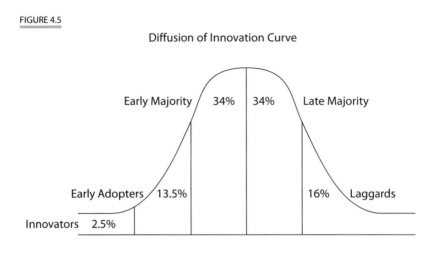

Diffusion of Innovation Curve

A recent example of how this curve works can be found in how use of the internet and the worldwide web diffused through our culture. In its early stage, only a few scientists in universities and the government used the internet, or even knew it existed. Then, commercial services like Compuserve and Prodigy became available, and early adopters came on-line. The introduction and massive marketing efforts of America On Line and the Microsoft Network attracted more and more users, until today, diffusion is solidly in the "late majority" stage, with only a small portion of the population having no internet access.

Using Consumer Models for Insight

With so many ways of looking at consumer behavior to consider, which model should you choose? The answer is different for every situation, but the question is one you should ask at the very start of a search for deeper insights. Thinking about consumer models can help guide you in a number of ways.

Beginning your examination of a new topic or product category with one or more behavioral models in mind is a good way to structure your thinking. A model can help identify aspects of the consumer's actions, attitudes, personality, lifestyle, or motivations that are most relevant to the product or problem you are considering. Using a model can help you set research objectives, and help you organize the findings of your observation and research in a meaningful way. A model "connects the dots" in a way that can paint a full and complete picture from individual bits and pieces of data.

Considering how more than one model might apply to your situation leads to triangulation, approaching the same problem from several different angles to come up with a fresher point of view. Deciding which model best explains how consumers process marketing information, which one gives a better understanding of their motivations and which model best describes their actions can lead to strategies that take into account all these dimensions, rather than just one.

Looking at a situation from a variety of angles can also help you put your marketing project into perspective. If you're the brand manager for Tide, selling soap is highly involving and deeply meaningful, but if you're the average purchaser, choosing a brand of laundry detergent may be a problem that comes up only once every few weeks and takes only a ten-second decision to resolve. Models that identify where and how a particular purchase fits into the consumer's life provide the most important insight of all.

SIX

How Consumers Think

EVERY DAY, most consumers are bombarded with a huge number of commercial messages and marketing appeals, from traditional TV and radio commercials to advertising placards on their grocery carts or product placements and sponsorships in virtually every form of commercial entertainment. How do these messages work? How do consumers process the information they receive, and how do marketing messages influence consumer choices? To understand these issues, it's important to know a little bit about how consumers think, that is, how our brains receive and process the endless stream of stimulating material in our surrounding environment.

For more than a century, scientists in a variety of disciplines have been trying to understand how human beings receive and process information, but until relatively recently, their work has been limited to what they could observe people saying and doing and the theories they could develop to explain that behavior. Over the past century, scientists and scholars in psychology, social psychology, communications theory, and cultural anthropology have all attempted to explain how people perceive and react to their environments.

In the last decade or so, Magnetic Resonance Imaging (MRI) has provided new avenues of investigation into the brain. For the first time ever, researchers can observe brain function directly, measuring where and how this complex organ responds to different forms of stimuli. The result has been a better understanding of some of the older theories, and development of whole new ideas into how the brain processes information. These new findings in neuropsychology help explain why some traditional marketing and advertising practices work, and why we are sometimes confused by the difference between what people say they think or feel and how they behave. Knowing more about how people think opens up new avenues to insight in every aspect of marketing.

There are several findings in neuropsychology that are relevant to marketing and advertising.

- We are not consciously aware of most of the activity that takes place in our brains. Researchers have stated that as much as 95 percent of all brain activity occurs below the level of conscious recognition, leaving a mere 5 percent open to examination by introspection and external questioning. Furthermore, even brain activity that qualifies as conscious may not be deeply reasoned or considered. Much is what researchers called heuristic thinking, a process that relies on superficial perception of symbolic cues and partial comprehension of messages, rather than on concentrated, active thought.

- In the way the brain functions, thoughts and emotions are not separate; they are intertwined. Basic instincts and emotions originate in the limbic system, a part of the brain that is common to all mammals. However, in humans, this instinctual center is closely linked to the parts of our brain that process cognitive thoughts, store memory, and make us capable of interpreting symbols and abstractions. The connection of instinctual and cognitive powers is what gives us control of our instinctive reactions and enables us to assign meaning to the physical sensations that we associate with emotion. In turn, our emotional reactions can influence our cognitive thoughts and memories, making it important to understand both the rational and emotional sides of human thought and behavior.

- Memory is the storage system for everything we know. Our brain's memory function is like a giant filing cabinet with three different kinds of files inside. One type includes all the procedures for action we have developed—how to walk, talk, sweep a floor, brush our teeth, or type words on a keyboard. The second holds our episodic memories, our experiences and the emotions and ideas we associate with them. Lastly, there is our semantic memory, which handles all the facts we have learned—the names of the state capitals, the idea that an open flame is too hot to touch, or the combination of sensations that we recognize as the taste of chocolate ice cream. When we "remember" something, we retrieve bits of information stored in individual brain cells, making electronic connections across the synapses or spaces between the cells. What we remember on any given occasion depends on the cues that prompt the memory. Different cues will activate different combinations of brain cells, resulting in retrieval of different bits of stored information, or different memories.

These findings are important because understanding how the brain works can help us identify the most appropriate ways to reach consumers with marketing messages. By examining how and when we consciously process information, and how and when we react to less conscious perceptions, we can tailor the appropriate kinds of messages to the situation we are trying to influence.

Conscious Thought versus Unconscious Perception

Long ago, psychologist Sigmund Freud understood that some beliefs, attitudes, and behaviors are the product of conscious thought while others may develop below the level of our conscious awareness. Recent studies have shown that even decisions we believe are conscious choices may be the result of pre-conscious recognition of the advantages and disadvantages of the alternatives we are considering. The brain activity related to making these choices occurs before we realize what we have decided. So, what you think you are thinking may not always be the whole truth.

When asked to describe "thinking," most of us will talk about a conscious, systematic thought process. We emphasize our efforts to rationally consider ideas presented to us, and our careful assessment of the meaning of arguments included in a message. You are probably engaged in this kind of thinking right now as you read this book and make an intentional effort to absorb the ideas presented.

Now take a moment to notice what else is going on around you. Are there other people present? Are they talking? What other sounds do you hear? Is there music playing, or perhaps an air conditioner producing a soft whirr of white noise? Is the room brightly lit, or a little dark? Are you seated comfortably, or do you need to get up and stretch your legs a little?

How aware of these surroundings were you before reading the previous paragraph forced you to concentrate on them? Most likely, you had a low level of consciousness of your environment, even though it was not the object of your primary focus. You knew whether or not other people were present, and probably noticed if they were talking, even if you were not fully tuned in to the conversation. You are also likely to have taken in other characteristics of the setting—the color or arrangement of the furniture, the noises, sights, and smells that were present, even though you were not intentionally noticing them.

The idea that we can be surrounded by a multitude of different stimuli and yet focus attention on only a small number of them—such as the markings that represent words on the page of this book—is known as selective perception. Most of the time, we are consciously aware and focused on only a limited number of the messages coming at us every minute, but even those we think we are ignoring may be having an effect on our brains and may get imprinted into our memories.

Unconscious Perception in Marketing

Most of the time, the marketing messages we are exposed to penetrate only the periphery of our consciousness. We tend to "tune out" advertising and other commercial messages, and the need to break through clutter and gain our attention is often assumed to be the first goal of advertising. However, even when a message fails to attract our conscious attention, we may perceive certain elements of it, calling on our ability to use cues to reduce the amount of information our brains need to process. Consumers rely on low-level perception rather than intense concentration to absorb messages as a strategy to process information with as little effort as possible. This thinking is what Krugman described in his consumer behavior model and what more recent authors, most notably, Robert Heath, have called low-involvement processing.

When we're in low-involvement mode, the brain takes in only a simplified version of what we are exposed to—basic concepts and perceptual memories such as sounds and shapes, rather than all the details. In marketing, this is enough to implant brand images and basic messages that are retained in memory, just waiting for the right cues to bring them to our conscious awareness. Low-involvement processing explains why measures of *advertising recognition* show higher awareness than measures of *recall*. The memories stored by low-involvement processing allow us to recognize what we've seen before, but when we receive messages in low-involvement mode, we miss the details needed to actively recall and repeat the message in the future.

Wendy Gordon, a leading British qualitative researcher, has written extensively about how the findings of neuropsychology inform our understanding of brands and branding. She describes a brand as "a dynamic and complex network of associations, built up through past experience," rather than a single complete image stored in memory. According to Gordon, even what we might call the components of a brand image, such as the logo, are broken into smaller pieces and stored in different brain cells. All the past experiences we've had with the brand are also retained separately—the advertising we've seen, the childhood memory of Mom buying and using the brand, even the vague perception of a lonely package on a dingy shelf in a tiny store in the small town where we went camping in the mountains five years ago.

When we consciously think of a brand, our brain connects some of the cells where these experiences are stored, and may ignore or leave out others, depending on the situation and the relevance of each individual encounter. The network of cells activated on one occasion is different from the network activated the next time the consumer thinks about the brand, and depends on the environmental cues that evoked the memory. If marketers are lucky, or better yet, smart, the brand messages they send to consumers will stimulate the more positive and favorable experiences, and leave the bad encounters undisturbed. We'll see the brand logo and think happy thoughts of Mom, not of the dingy camp store or the leaky package that made a mess in the refrigerator.

Because everyone has more associations with a specific brand than any single situation evokes, and because the associations stored in each consumer's brain are unique to his or her own experiences, no two consumers have exactly the same mental image of a brand, and even in the same consumer, images will shift depending on the cues present in the environment. That's why it is important to be consistent and purposeful in all the messages about a brand that you can control. Marketing, customer service, operations, and all other parts of the company must conduct their activities in a way that reinforces brand messages the organization wants to send and avoids evoking negative associations consumers may have picked up on their own. Consumer insights can guide this effort by using research to reveal the positive and negative associations in consumer memory, finding cues to evoke desirable feelings and motivate action.

Using Cues to Influence Consumer Behavior

Sensory cues evoke memories and brand images, sometimes very powerfully. Visualize a set of three concentric circles—an inner red dot surrounded by a white ring, which is in turn surrounded by another red one. When you evoke this image, what else comes to mind? In some situations, you might call this symbol a bulls-eye, but if you see it on the side of a building or in a newspaper, you're more likely to recognize it as the logo for Target Stores. Target has linked this image with its name so successfully that its advertising featuring the logo never has to mention the store name. The cue of the red and white circles is powerful enough to make us "fill in" the missing identity of the advertiser.

It's well-known that olfactory cues can influence purchase behavior. Supermarkets use the smell of freshly baked bread to draw customers to the in-store bakery, and some fast food addicts are irresistibly drawn to the smell of McDonald's French fries. Bad smells can turn consumers away, while certain good ones can reinforce claims of freshness, efficacy or power.

Perceptual cues help us make decisions before we realize we have done so. Unconscious or pre-conscious processing of our surroundings can help us decide that one brand is "higher quality" than another, or that a medical expert is "authoritative" or a car salesman is "friendly." Cues that create these feelings or intuitions are present, even if consumers are not consciously aware of them. Understanding how cues work allows us to structure the purchase situation and make the sale more effectively.

Cialdini's Six Principles of Persuasion

Robert Cialdini, Ph.D., is a prominent social psychologist who has written extensively on the use of cues to achieve persuasion, based on his own research and the research of others studying the topic of influence. To learn more about how persuasion works, Cialdini worked in sales jobs in a number of different industries, as well as in advertising, public relations, and fund-raising. By combining his observation of which techniques and cues work in these situations with the findings of social science researchers studying persuasion in academic settings, he identified six principles of influence that work in a broad range of situations.

The six principles are scarcity, reciprocation, commitment and consistency, social proof, liking, and authority. These principles are the foundations of almost all sales and marketing approaches developed over the years. Using consumer insights research to learn which of these principles is most likely to be effective, and how to shape the strategy developed to reach the consumer, can be a powerful path to marketing success.

The Principle of Scarcity

"Last chance." "Limited edition." "One-time only offer."

These common sales pitches rely upon the principle of scarcity, which says that people always want something more if they know they cannot have it or if the supply of it is rare or hard to find. In the 1980s, anxious parents lined up at Christmas time to buy Cabbage Patch dolls for children who today, as adults, line up with their own children to buy the latest Harry Potter book the day it hits the bookstores. In hot real estate markets, sellers ask potential buyers to accompany their full-price offer with a letter to the owner outlining why they "deserve" the house they seek. In the world of consumer marketing, disruptions in supply are accompanied with full-page newspaper ads apologizing for the shortage, making low-fat cookies or miracle skin creams even more desirable because they have become impossible to find.

Under normal marketing conditions, where supplies are plentiful and consumers have plenty of choices, the underlying principle of scarcity can still influence consumer behavior. Research has shown that people almost automatically fight against restrictions to their freedom; as early as the "terrible twos," children start to know what they want and know how to get it. As adults, being told something is "not available" makes us just as anxious to have it as a two-year-old denied a toy—although by adulthood, we have usually developed better coping strategies than the two-year-old who throws a temper tantrum in the middle of the shopping mall. We line up before dawn the day after Thanksgiving to get the bargain price on a new TV set or DVD player at Wal-Mart, and then spend the rest of the morning shopping off the previous day's pumpkin pie. We stock up on milk and bread if a snowstorm threatens to limit our future trip to the grocery store. We bid more than we intend to at auctions. We want what we cannot get immediately, even if it is objectively less appealing than an available alternative.

To build a marketing strategy on the principle of scarcity, consumer insights research is needed to determine what consumers value, and what they fear they will lose if they cannot make a purchase. Parents who desperately shopped for those Cabbage Patch dolls were not just looking for attractive, appropriate playthings for their children. If that's what they had wanted, there were hundreds of other choices available. Those who searched from store to store or paid twice the normal price did so because only a genuine Cabbage Patch doll would prove their parental love and "save" the family Christmas.

The Principle of Reciprocation

The principle of reciprocation is that we always try to repay in kind what another person provides us. Hare Krishnas handing out flowers in an airport before asking travelers for money use this principle, as do direct-mail fundraisers who include personalized address labels in their charitable requests. Politicians try to secure our support in the next election through constituent services. In my hometown, Chicago, that might mean a new garbage can from a local precinct captain, while on a national scale, we re-elect Congressmen who "bring home the bacon" from pork-barrel projects that benefit our local districts.

In marketing, giving away free samples is one way to generate future sales, especially in a one-to-one sales situation. A new car salesman is likely to offer a prospective buyer coffee or a soft drink before sitting down to write up a cost proposal. Your neighborhood Avon or Amway representative may drop by with a goodie bag of trial products, all with no obligation, of course. Some marketers provide the gift of information, in the form of recipes, travel-planning guides, or other service materials they hope will eventually lead to a purchase. Consultative selling depends on the principle of reciprocation. In a high-stakes business situation, the vendor's representative may provide highly valuable "free" consulting services directed at the potential customer's business problem for weeks or months before attempting a serious sales pitch, while at the department store cosmetics counter, the salesperson offers a "free" make-over as a prelude to the sale.

These techniques all work, but more subtle and sophisticated reciprocation techniques may work even more effectively. One method Cialdini calls "rejection then retreat" sets up a situation in which the potential customer is presented with an offer or request he is likely to turn down. Following the turn-down, the seller comes back with a lesser offer, essentially conceding victory to the buyer on the first exchange, and thereby setting up a situation in which the buyer must make a reciprocal concession in order to even out the relationship. The lesser offer may be the deal the seller always intended to make, but the buyer goes along simply because he turned down the earlier, more extravagant proposal. This is a standard technique in negotiation, but it also applies in many other situations. Your insurance agent probably uses it when he calls to ask if you would like to increase coverage or add a new policy. If you refuse that offer, he's almost certain to ask if you can give him the names of a few friends who might be interested in his services.

Cialdini even uses the Reciprocation Principle to explain the Nixon administration's decision to approve the Watergate break-in that eventually led to its downfall. After two much more outrageous schemes proposed by G. Gordon Liddy were turned down by the President's advisors, the request for authorization to plant listening devices in Democratic Party headquarters seemed like a concession on his part, and those in charge felt an obligation to reciprocate, much to their later regret.

The Principle of Commitment and Consistency

The principle of commitment and consistency says that we want to be consistent with what we have already done, and to appear consistent to others. This idea is the basis for the theory of cognitive dissonance, that says we try so hard to be consistent that we can be induced to change our beliefs to match our behavior when the two are in opposition.

Sales people use this principle when they ask easy-to-agree-to qualifying questions before asking for the sale. After all, if we are the type of parent who wants our child to do well in school, and we believe that students need access to the best available technology, and we are willing to put our child's needs ahead of other considerations, why wouldn't we want to buy her a spanking new computer with all the technological bells and whistles? We are, after all, parents who make sure our children have everything they need to succeed.

One of the most important aspects of the commitment and consistency principle is that we use perceptions of ourselves as a way to simplify decision-making. When we tell ourselves, "I'm a person who . . . ," we are well on our way to making a whole host of decisions without having to process a lot of information. If my self perception is "I'm a chocoholic," it's easy to pick the most elaborate chocolate concoction on the menu for dessert. If it's "I'm a Democrat," or "I'm a Republican," my reaction to a particular political question may be fixed long before I've heard and understood all the arguments for and against my position. If I tell others "I'm going to quit smoking," I'm less likely to light up, at least in public.

In the marketing world, simplified decision-making based on consistency and commitment affects all kinds of consumer choices. A "Mac person" is unlikely to be a good target for a new Windows-based computer. A "good mother" is a great prospect for all kinds of products to enhance the health, safety, and well-being of children. A "gourmet cook" will respond to food products very differently from the person who says her most developed cooking skill is using the kitchen phone to order takeout.

Another aspect of the commitment and consistency principle is that taking one action can influence future behavior. An art lover previously content with reproductions buys an expensive oil painting, and soon finds herself going to art fairs and art galleries, buying other paintings and subscribing to art magazines, because she is now "a person who buys art." A former couch potato signs up to run in a charity race and finds himself joining a gym and watching his diet in addition to following the prescribed training routine. One action triggers a series of other behaviors, which in turn, can change self-perception and influence decisions in the future.

Investigating the self-images and values consumers hold and how a product either enhances or detracts from them is an essential foundation for marketing. The most powerful insight is to find the connection between the commitments consumers make—to themselves and to others—and what your brand can do to help enhance their self-perceptions.

The Principle of Social Proof

One way we determine what is important, appropriate or correct is to consider what others like us are thinking and doing. This principle is what makes TV producers use laugh tracks in their programs, and what prompts bartenders or church ushers to "salt" the tip jar or collection plate with a few high-value bills. It's what makes us look around to see what others are doing before we help a person in distress on a crowded street, and what transforms ordinarily law-abiding sports fans into a roving mob of trouble-makers when their team wins or loses a championship game.

In marketing, social proof is the principle behind "man-on-the-street" testimonials or claims that "more mothers choose" a brand. It works best when the people we use as models are "like us" rather than strange, different or foreign. So, Dove uses "average women" instead of glamorous models to promote its skin care products. Door-to-door insurance salesmen in rural areas bring along a ring binder containing the names and addresses of local farmers who have purchased the same policies. Advertisers targeting ethnic audiences not only cast ethnically appropriate actors for their commercials, but also make sure that the settings and situations reflect the lifestyle of the group they are trying to reach.

An important task for consumer insights researchers is learning about the peer groups that target consumers look to for guidance. This is especially important when the target is different from most marketing decision-makers, well-educated professional business people who live a typically well-heeled, middle-class life. To step outside our own frame of reference, and into the shoes of an urban teenager, a small-town business owner, or a hard-working truck driver with three kids and a second mortgage, we need to learn everything we can about that person before we can put social proof strategies into action.

The Principle of Liking

It's a well-accepted idea that we are more likely to be persuaded by someone we like than by someone we dislike. However, in a marketing situation, what are the factors that make someone or something more likeable than the competition? What elements of personality, appearance or presentation can tip the scale in our favor?

Physical attractiveness has been found to greatly increase liking. A considerable body of research has shown that, all else being equal, the better-looking candidate gets more votes, more attractive defendants get lighter sentences, and cuter kids get better treatment from teachers. That's why beautiful models are an advertising staple, and why a "Brand X" user might be depicted as less attractive or even a little goofy. We want to associate our brand with the more appealing person, and our competitors with the less liked individual.

Similarity also promotes liking, whether the common factor is an opinion, a personality trait, or a common background or lifestyle. Good sales people always look for a way to make "small talk" that establishes a common bond with the potential customer, before launching into a sales pitch. Marketers establish similarity by finding something that makes the product a good fit with the intended target audience.

Similarity in dress and other external cues can be important. In the 1950s, ads for household cleaning products featured models dressed in high heels and pearls. Today, they're more likely to show an attractive, but not too attractive, thirty-something actress in jeans, in an appealing, but not too fancy home that looks something like the consumer's own environment.

Familiarity and cooperative contact are also ways to foster liking. In the "good-cop, bad-cop" scenario, the good cop puts himself on the side of the suspect, supposedly working against his own bad-cop partner, and forges a bond that eventually works against the suspect's interests. Marketing messages that tell the target that "we're on your side" or "we're all working toward the same thing" can develop the same kind of trusting relationship, presumably with a better ultimate outcome for the customer.

Conditioning and association are the ways the principle of liking works to create positive or negative feelings toward brands and companies. When two objects are paired, we transfer our feelings toward one to the other as well. That's why we often blame the weatherman for bad weather and actors who play villains on television are sometimes accosted on the street by angry fans. In marketing, we try to minimize the negative reactions to things we associate with our brand, and maximize the positives. It's why we use celebrity spokespeople, and tie-ins with the Olympics, local sports teams, or well-respected charities and cultural associations. Marketing can also associate brands with popular ideas or trends, such as promoting a particular food as ideal for those on the latest fad diet.

When liking is a possible strategy, research can guide decision-makers to the most appropriate role models and associations. Identifying the right cues to reach target consumers can be the insight that makes a campaign successful.

The Principle of Authority

Cialdini's final element of influence is the principle of authority, which says that people will follow the direction of those they believe to be more knowledgeable or of higher status than themselves.

This is the foundation for the effectiveness of expert recommendations, scientific proof and even the approach that says "I'm not a doctor, but I play one on TV." When consumers feel comfortable with the superior knowledge, expertise, or status of someone recommending a product, that cue alone can make them choose it over other alternatives.

There are a multitude of advertising and marketing efforts based on the principle of authority, but these attempts are not always successful with today's media-savvy consumers. We've become too sophisticated to be fooled by an actor in a white coat, but other aspects of authority are still remarkably effective. "Seals of Approval," or scientific evidence from an authoritatively named source can convey a strong message, as can a spokesperson's appearance, title, clothing, environment, or manner. Research that investigates consumer reactions generated by potential sources of authority and expertise can provide useful insights to guide the creators of these messages.

SEVEN

How Consumers Talk

UNDERSTANDING how consumers talk is at least as important as understanding how they think. Thought and language are connected by an ever-repeating feedback loop. Not only do our thoughts determine what we say, but the way we express and communicate our ideas shapes the way we think about the world. Understanding and insight must take into account not just what consumers say, but what their language choices reveal about their innermost feelings and reactions.

To fully understand the meaning behind consumer words, you must become sensitive to the nuances of speech. Look at the ways people use figurative language. Notice how people use stories. Watch for how the psychological phenomenon of projection affects what people say and how they say it, and consider the way men and women typically express themselves when you look for either similarities or differences between the sexes.

Metaphor as a Mirror of the Mind

One of the most important aspects of language is the use of figurative speech that expresses one idea in terms of another. Traditionally, scholars have looked upon figurative or metaphorical language as mere poetic license, a departure from the literal meaning of words used to add interest or color to speech and writing. More recent theories, however, describe metaphorical thinking as a basic cognitive process, a way in which our brains connect one idea to another.

These "cross-domain mappings" are revealed when we use figurative language—metaphorical expressions using words, phrases, sentences, or whole stories to describe the associations our minds have made.

If we think of metaphor as a way of conceptualizing, rather than as just a figure of speech, then noticing the metaphors people use to express their ideas helps us understand how they organize their thoughts, feelings, attitudes, and beliefs on the subject we are investigating.

Within any culture, many metaphorical structures will be held in common. Some are so widely held and so deeply entrenched that we don't even notice them as metaphorical. When we say, for example, that "time passes" or "the time will come," we are conceptualizing time in terms of motion through space. In one version of this metaphor, individual bits of time are things, constantly in motion around us as fixed observers. We talk about time as "in front of us" in the future or "behind us" in the past. We "look ahead" to an upcoming event, bemoan the fact that "time flies" when we are enjoying ourselves, and tell our children that "the time will come" when they understand our parental concerns. In a variation of this metaphor, we are the object in motion, passing by fixed elements of time. So, we say "he passed the time anxiously" or "we're coming up on the holidays," to express our ideas of temporal progression.

Similarly, a common idea within our culture is that "life is a journey," where our goals are "destinations" and the obstacles we encounter are "bumps in the road." If we become diverted from our objective, we say we have "taken a wrong turn," or "gone down the wrong path," and if we can't decide what we want to do next, we say we're "at a crossroads" in our thinking.

In consumer language, metaphors express the relationships people have with the products they use. When a man describes his latest electronic gadget as a "daddy toy," he's expressing a different relationship to the product than the fellow who calls the same device his "favorite tool." When one person says that mopping the kitchen floor feels "like I'm in the Navy or something, swabbing the deck," but another says "floor cleaning is my therapy," you're hearing about different rewards that can be derived from this routine household chore.

Consumers also use metaphors to describe their needs and feelings. Some young adults talk about their credit cards as "a key" that opens up opportunities they otherwise could not take advantage of, like travel or education. Others will set one card aside as a "safety net" that is always available for use in emergencies. Some like to use credit or debit cards as a "bookkeeper" that lets them see exactly how they spend their money. And, to many, the credit card can be "a raging beast" they must control so it does not become "a ball and chain" when they spend too freely and run up balances they have a hard time paying off.

Paying attention to metaphors can reveal "hidden negatives" or warning signals in consumer comments. If consumers say your package design looks "rich and luxurious, like a family heirloom," they are giving positive feedback, but you may need to rethink the idea of positioning the product as an up-to-the-minute technological breakthrough. If people describe your new cleaning tool as "a scooter, that's quick and light, and goes wherever you want," you probably have a lock on a convenience claim, but may have a hard time convincing people to use your brand for heavy-duty jobs.

The metaphors consumers use also illuminate the values they associate with a particular brand or product category. Respondents who called a brand "the Aunt Bea of all companies," were expressing nostalgia, familiarity, and a non-challenging domesticity personified by the motherly TV-character from *The Andy Griffith Show,* set in 1950s. These feelings were a sharp contrast to their feelings toward the brand they called "more like Martha Stewart," which, they explained, is impressive and stylish, but also difficult to use, more expensive, and more likely to make their friends think they are "showing off."

When looking for insights, give your target audience the opportunity to express themselves metaphorically. Use interviewing techniques like the ones described in Chapter 9 to bring out verbal and visual metaphors related to your product category or brand. Once you've

identified the metaphors consumers use, extend them. Use them to
broaden and energize your own thinking, your own understanding
and your own insight.

Advertising for the prescription anti-depressant Zoloft did just
that. Feelings of sadness are commonly described as "being low" or
"under a cloud." So, Zoloft showed a cute little cartoon character,
feeling depressed at the bottom of a hole, with Zoloft as the ladder
providing a means of escape. In another ad, the character was rescued
from falling rain by his Zoloft umbrella. In a dark cave, Zoloft was
the light that brightened up the day. By extending the depression
metaphor, Zoloft conveyed its benefit to consumers in a meaningful
and entertaining way, even within the strict regulations governing
advertising for prescription drugs.

Projection Lets Consumers Keep Their Distance

The psychological principle of Pprojection says that people may
unconsciously assume that others share the same thoughts, feelings,
beliefs or perceptions on any given topic as they do. Psychologists
view this phenomenon as a defense mechanism. People project "bad"
or socially unacceptable feelings of their own onto others, and thus
are able to express themselves without having to take ownership or
responsibility for their thoughts.

In consumer insights, it is important to be aware of this tendency
when interpreting what consumers have to say about a topic or product, especially when you ask them to talk about highly personal,
unpleasant, or socially unacceptable actions and ideas. You can also
take advantage of projection, and use it as a technique to gain a better understanding of the individual consumer's true feelings in situations where he or she is reluctant to express them.

Careful listening will help you identify projection and differentiate it from a true report of the behavior or feelings of "other people"
the consumer might want to tell you about. When consumers want
to convey something about other people with whom they are familiar, they will tend to talk in very specific terms. They'll tell you, "My
brother-in-law says . . . " or "A guy I work with told me . . ." Or

they will be general, but personal, making statements such as "Most people I know feel . . ." or "I've heard a lot of people say . . ."

When people are projecting, they are trying to distance themselves from the thought they are expressing, so they are more likely to talk in general and impersonal terms. When someone says, "People say Brand X doesn't work" or "Some people might be afraid of the chemicals in this food," there is probably an element of personal belief or feeling in the statement, even though the speaker is uncomfortable admitting to it.

Most of the time, consumers will project their thoughts and feelings onto other people, but they can also avoid giving direct criticism by projecting onto another place or usage situation. It's a common joke among focus group moderators that when focus group participants enthusiastically tell you that a new product "would be good for camping," the probability of its success is close to zero. Similarly, when respondents over forty say "younger people might like this," or teenagers say, "maybe my parents would buy it," what they're really saying is "this product holds no interest for me."

When consumers start talking this way, don't challenge the statement or try to pin down the "source" of their information or the evidence for their belief. You'll just increase the level of discomfort, and shut down the discussion entirely. Instead, react with interest and curiosity, and let the consumer develop the idea further. You're more likely to get the insight you need.

When a consumer says, "Some people might be too lazy to recycle," respond with a comment like, "That's interesting. What do you suppose makes people lazy about recycling?" This probe might reveal the consumer's distrust of the local community's recycling system, or the household's lack of space for separate recycling bins, or the consumer's reluctance to "nag" other family members into separating their trash. Because the principle of projection is that people attribute their own motivations and beliefs to others, these responses will move you closer to understanding what to do to address the issue. By letting the consumer maintain and extend the projection, you go deeper into his or her own motivations and barriers.

Men and Women Each Speak Their Own Genderlects

The issue of communication, or the lack of it, between men and women has provided material for an endless line of stand-up comedians, and fills the appointment calendars of marriage counselors everywhere. It may be just a joke to say that each sex has its own language, but linguistics experts studying this problem have concluded that men and women really do have different ways of speaking, which they have named the **genderlect** styles.

Paying attention to genderlect will help you communicate better with both men and women, and get to deeper insights you can use with both sexes. Sometimes you will find that although men and women speak differently, they are expressing the same feelings, needs, and motivations. In other situations, you may be hearing the same words, but the meaning behind them is different. To really understand, go beyond speaking style to get to the meaning of what consumers of both genders have to say.

Because speech patterns reflect both biological and cultural influences, including gender, not all men speak exactly the same way, nor do all women. However, men use some patterns of speech more regularly whereas women use others. Cultural and social norms probably account for the greatest degree of difference, although recent discoveries in brain research show that some differences in male and female speech reflect inherent differences in biology.

When you talk to consumers, take into account the differences between men and women, both in how you structure the conversation and in how you interpret what is said. This is especially important when interviewing or observing consumers in group settings, because many differences in genderlect stem from the way men and women typically interact with others.

Keep in mind that men typically use a speaking style that establishes dominance—their status position in the social structure. In the extreme, men who use this pattern treat conversation as a competition that all speakers are trying to "win." Each speaker tries to maintain control of the discussion and win over the other participants, without succumbing to their influence. Men compete for the floor; they interrupt each other freely and they are comfortable stating their opinions authoritatively, even when they are unsure of how they really think or feel.

When you talk with male consumers, take these tendencies into account. In a group setting, allow plenty of time for each person to speak, perhaps even reducing the size of the group to do so. Ask male consumers to play devil's advocate for the positions they initially take to force them to explore an issue completely. Ask them to identify problems and find solutions. They will take on the challenge and do their best to attain whatever goal you set for them.

At the same time, remember that men are usually uneasy talking about feelings or emotion. If your goal is to learn about emotions and get behind the public face of your consumers, think about how to get around this barrier. One tactic might be to conduct individual interviews, rather than try to explore emotional topics in a group setting. Another might be to use a variety of projective techniques that give your male respondents a way to talk about their feelings without having to admit to them.

Women, in contrast, look at conversation as a way to build rapport and connection. They look for common ground and shared understanding, while avoiding conflict and dissent. They take responsibility for what goes wrong. If a woman is dissatisfied with the way a product works, she's as likely to blame herself as she is to think there's something wrong with the product. In a taste test, for instance, a man might say "this product is too bland," while a woman with the same reaction to the product might comment, "I can't taste the spices."

When a woman makes what sounds like a statement of fact, she may be expressing an intention or expectation or even giving a direct order. In a work situation, a female executive might tell her assistant that "we'll need copies of this report for the meeting," and feel that she has clearly directed the subordinate to make the copies. With consumers, a parallel might be the restaurant patron who tells a server,

"It's a little noisy in here," with the full expectation that the volume of background music will be lowered.

A group of women with strong female genderlect will seek a way to come to consensus, rather than accept differences in their attitudes and feelings. In some situations, this search for common ground might be just what you need, but in other cases, you'll miss the full range of reactions, as the group participants who disagree with the most dominant speakers may stay silent or give up their contrary position in favor of cooperation.

To avoid being taken in by the genderlect of female research subjects, stress the importance of the individual's unique perspective. In a group, get individuals to commit to an opinion silently, by writing something down or making a personal choice, before sharing ideas with others. Make note of what might seem like casual comments or tentative opinions, because they could be revelations of stronger reactions and expectations. Provide a safe and comfortable platform for criticism and negative comments. Ask for ideas to "improve" or "fix" what's wrong with the product or idea. Have individuals work together in teams to build on each other's suggestions.

When your target audience includes both men and women, look for ways to combine the speaking styles of both genders in your communications and marketing efforts. Rely on one style or the other and you run the risk of being misunderstood by half your audience. Use genderlects wisely and you will reach both men and women more effectively.

Storytelling Orders the Universe

One of the most valuable ways to get consumers to communicate their thoughts and to reveal how they structure their ideas is to ask them to tell stories. We all grew up with "Once upon a time" fairy tales and innately respond to messages with a beginning, a middle, and an end. We expect certain outcomes. Good triumphs over evil. Persistence pays off. Hard work leads to success. When asked to recount an experience, we provide a narrative—first I did this. Then, this happened. A problem arose. I struggled. I found a solution. We lived happily ever after. The end.

In recent years, marketers have learned that telling a story to consumers is almost always an effective way to communicate. People get involved in narratives, connect to the emotional elements, and remember what the story had to say about the brand. Presenting marketing messages through storytelling is a powerful technique.

Listening to the stories consumers tell can be even more enlightening. When consumers tell stories involving the brands and products they use, they reveal more about their lives and their feelings than they overtly recount. Asking consumers to tell the story of their last experience with a brand provides detail and context that simply asking them what they know or feel about the brand does not. In telling their stories, consumers will tell you the situations and settings in which they use the brand. They will describe the social and environmental triggers that evoke thoughts of the brand or that create a need for the benefit the brand provides. They'll talk about the outcome, how the brand satisfied their need, or how it disappointed them, or what would have made the experience more meaningful. They create heroes and villains, they describe problems and struggles, and they tell you what they were thinking and feeling along the way. Listen for the insight and you'll rarely be disappointed.

Storytelling as an interviewing technique is especially useful when you are exploring a long or complicated process that takes place over time or involves a cast of characters beyond the individual consumer or buyer. Going through the process in story form lets the consumer reconstruct the experience in a systematic way, adding whatever he or she has learned in the meantime. A story of a personal experience is not just an historical account; it's a revelation of where the storyteller stands right now, how previous experiences have influenced the present situation, and what might happen differently in the future.

Want to know about new car buying? Don't ask consumers about features and benefits, or about which brands they like and dislike, or any of the traditional kinds of questions you might see on a typical research survey. Instead, ask them to tell you the story of the last car they bought—what made them decide they needed or wanted a new car, what they did about it, where they shopped, who went with them, what problems or obstacles they ran in to, what encounters they had with sales people or others involved in the process, what made them pick the car they bought, how they negotiated the deal, and how they felt when they finally took possession of their new vehicle. In ten or fifteen minutes, you'll know how that consumer approaches car buying. In ten or fifteen interviews, you'll have a deeper understanding of your marketplace.

Want to understand how individual family members influence the purchase of bottled salad dressing? Don't ask who influences the purchase. Ask what happens when salad is served at a family dinner. How is the salad prepared? What ingredients are included? Who decides what to put in? When does the dressing go on? Who chooses that? What happens next? How does the storyteller feel? What makes everyone live "happily ever after?" What happens when the story doesn't turn out so well?

When listening to consumer stories, deconstruct what they say, and look for the structural elements of the narrative. Notice the basic plot of the story and what drives the action. Is it a quest, with a hero who goes in search of something, overcoming a series of obstacles before attaining the goal? Is it a story of grief and loss? Is love or hate a dominant theme? Are the story characters fulfilling ambitions, seeking revenge or dealing with a catastrophe? Is there a rivalry or betrayal? Does the story include mistaken identities or result in a reversal of fortune?

Who are the main characters? Notice whether your product is the hero or the villain or just an incidental agent without a central role in the plot. If the product is not important to the story, it's a signal that it could easily be replaced by another brand or even some other item. Notice the role the storyteller assigns to him or herself. What does that tell you about the consumer's relationship to the product category or brand? What insight does it reveal?

Are there any symbolic elements in the story, objects or characters that have deeper meaning for the storyteller or consumer? Are these meanings a result of the marketing cues you have provided, or do they come from other aspects of the consumer's life? If they come from sources you can't control, what can you do to shape the story your way?

What are the opposing forces that provide conflict and drama? Look for the climax of the story. What happens to resolve the conflict? How do the characters change as a result? Does the product contribute to a favorable resolution? Can you do something to give it more power in the situation?

In your analysis, think about the beliefs the story is based on, what facts the storyteller includes, and what feelings he or she reveals. Look for the social norms and expectations that drive the story, and how your brand, your message, and your marketing efforts relate to these norms. Consider whether your product fills an expected role, or goes against convention.

In your own quest for insight, let consumer stories lead the way. Search for ways your brand or product helps the consumer get to a favorable outcome. If that's not the role consumers give your product, think about what your marketing can do to help the story turn out more positively. Find the elements of your brand story that give consumers a better story to tell, and you'll all live happily ever after. The end.

Part III

Moving from Research Toward Insight

EIGHT

Techniques for Understanding Lives and Lifestyles

AN IMPORTANT DIFFERENCE between consumer insights and traditional marketing research is that the insight-driven approach emphasizes the need for putting product-specific information into the context of the consumer's overall life and lifestyle. Studies rich with insights are rarely limited to analysis of product features and benefits, brand-specific attitudes, or category usage habits. These issues are important, but the most revealing research is typically broader in scope. To generate new insight, you need to look at the environment in which the product is sold and consumed, the other choices consumers make in the same context, and the importance or value they place on these decisions. In other words, to fully understand your category and market, you must put the product into the context of the consumer's whole experience.

A Wider Lens Captures More

If you are trying to find a new positioning for your particular brand of toothpaste, you won't have the time, budget or inclination to investigate the complete life histories of your consumers or to document every aspect of daily activities, but you should look beyond product features and benefits or the images of your brand and its major competitors. Instead of limiting your research to toothpaste-related topics, it might be productive to look at feelings and attitudes toward personal grooming, parental concerns about developing good habits in their children, beliefs about preventive health care, or even reactions to bright, shiny faces and toothy grins. In other words, if you are looking for insights, it helps to back up a couple of steps and let some of the surroundings intrude into your picture.

Studying the broader context might mean learning everything you can about how your target consumer thinks, feels and behaves, or it might mean understanding the marketplace trends that can influence whether potential consumers recognize a need for your product, how they learn that it exists, and what benefits they expect it to provide. It may require you to figure out how consumers' ethnic backgrounds influence their product choices, or even their behavior in a research setting. You might have to take into account the different needs and motivations experienced by consumers with different family structures or lifestyles, investigate whether gender differences play a part, or think about how regional conditions or other geographic factors affect the marketplace in which you operate.

Understanding the broader context may also mean studying other participants in the marketing process that link you to the consumer, such as the distributors, retailers, delivery services, technical support people, or perceived experts who may not be under your control but who may greatly influence consumer choices. If you're engaged in multinational marketing, you'll also need to take into account how culture, tradition, law, competitive environment, and consumer characteristics vary from country to country, or even from region-to-region within the United States, and what these differences mean for your marketing program.

Start with Personal Immersion

To understand more about your target audience, begin with some **personal immersion**. Put yourself in your target's environment and experience some of the pleasures they enjoy or the daily challenges they must face. You'll come away with a better perspective on your product and where it fits into the consumer's bigger picture. Sometimes you can only partially relate to your target audience's life, but even partial immersion can be helpful.

If you're forty years old and can't even remember the name of your date to the senior prom, you obviously can't become a 14-year-old. However, you can read a few issues of *Seventeen, Cosmo Girl,* or *Teen People.* You can log on to some websites teenagers are likely to frequent. You can listen to the latest boy bands or hip-hop artists, and you can make it a habit to stroll through teen-oriented departments and shops at the mall, just to see what's on display.

If you're an affluent professional living in a trendy urban neighborhood, you can't become a small-town business owner. However, you can put on some casual clothes, drive to a small town, hang out in a local diner at lunch time, stop in a few stores on Main Street, take a look at the new Wal-Mart on the outskirts of town and begin to get a feeling for the differences between your outlook and your target audience's.

Visit stores where your product is sold, or watch your consumers wherever they encounter your product. Fieldwork in a variety of locations will give you an understanding of your products and customers that the view from headquarters cannot possibly reveal. If you are in the hotel industry, visit your own as well as competing hotels frequently, and don't always identify yourself as a corporate insider. If you work in a museum, get out of your office in the hidden-away back corner of the building and spend time on the exhibition floor. Whatever your business, put yourself in the situation and environment where your product meets its buyers and users on a regular basis.

When you are in observation mode, be alert to the details around you. Look at how your customers are dressed; who they are with; how they walk through the site; how they interact with each other, with the staff, and with the products they buy or reject. Try to guess how people are feeling. Are they happy and relaxed? Tense? In a hurry? Confused? What is causing these reactions? What could be done to make them more comfortable? What could make the experience more efficient? How could customers be more completely satisfied?

If there are intermediaries between you and the end buyer or consumer, visit and be familiar with every link in the chain. Meet with your wholesalers and distributors. Get to know your franchisees and include visits to some of the less successful operators, not just the big guns on your franchisee council. If you supply an industrial product purchased by corporate buyers who never even see what they buy, ask to talk to workers who actually use what you sell in their jobs.

Beyond these more or less informal site visits, you can also conduct formal in-home or ethnographic interviews to get more deeply into the question of how your product fits into the consumer's everyday life.

In consumer insights, **in-home visits** are qualitative interviews conducted in the consumer's home to allow for a more up-close and personal view of your subject. Typically, you'll arrange appointments with target consumers at times appropriate for the product you're studying. If your product is a breakfast cereal, you'll want to be in the home when the family is eating breakfast. If it's a household cleaner, you'll want to go while the kids are in school and the homemaker is in her cleaning mode, or in the evening to talk to working people. A gardening product or do-it-yourself tools may require weekend visits when these kinds of projects are typically undertaken. Plan to spend several hours in each home, so you'll have plenty of time to learn about the household in general as well as to cover the topic you are studying.

Going directly to where consumers live can yield insight and information you can obtain no other way. Asking a respondent to tell you how she sorts laundry or what steps are involved in preparing rice will never yield the details you will notice when you watch several consumers actually perform these tasks on their own turf. Survey questions about storage problems, competitive product use, or the influence of children on the family's choice of salad dressings will never be as interesting or as revealing as seeing for yourself how your target consumers handle these issues. And imagine you're looking for a reaction to several prototype designs for a new floor mop. Would you rather have respondents come to a central research facility and try the new mops on a small piece of flooring artificially dirtied especially for the occasion, or would their reactions be more realistic at home, testing the mops on their own floors, with their own individual varieties of dirt?

Each of these situations can be the opportunity for an in-home visit that can also give you a more meaningful picture of how target consumers live, and how your product fits into their everyday routines. While you are in their homes, asking specific questions about the topic at hand, you'll also absorb impressions and ideas about the family and the surroundings that can lead to deeper insights and a better interpretation of your basic findings.

Setting up and carrying out in-home interviews takes extra planning, but need not be more costly than focus groups or other types of qualitative research. Many research firms that recruit and host focus groups can also set up in-home interviews for you, for about the same cost as the equivalent number of interviews conducted at their facilities.

If possible, use a local firm for recruiting your in-home respondents, because recruiters familiar with the area will be able to create a route for your travels that takes into account not just the distance between households but traffic conditions, school hours, and other factors that will affect travel time or respondent availability.

Recruiters typically pre-screen in-home respondents using the same criteria they would use for a focus group, but provide additional information to reassure the consumer about the strangers who will be visiting her home. The screening process should include a description of what the interview will entail. If you want respondents to do laundry or cook rice for you, tell them so in advance. Tell them whether you will be bringing a product for them to try, or if you'll want them to use the product they have on hand. Tell them you'll want to look inside kitchen cabinets and refrigerators, or visit the family's bedrooms, or the storage shed in the back yard, or anyplace else a typical guest in the home would not have access to. If you want to tape record or take photographs or video of the visit, inform respondents during the screening process, and let them know you'll be asking them to sign a release that gives permission for these activities.

Keep the visit as informal as possible. Dress casually, as you would for an informal visit to a personal acquaintance. Designate one person as the main interviewer for each visit, and limit additional assistants to only one or two observers, each of whom should have some task to perform, such as operating a video camera or taking notes.

A home visit is a very personal encounter, so you won't be able to maintain total anonymity. The recruiters should give respondents the name of the person who will be conducting the interview as well as an explanation of who else will be in the group. You don't have to identify your company or client, if disclosing this information will bias the interview. Instead, introduce yourself as someone who works with the company who did the recruiting, so respondents have a legitimate, established business they can check out if they have doubts or questions.

The recruiter should provide you with a phone number for each respondent and clear directions to each home. If you are interviewing in an unfamiliar area, it may be worthwhile to hire a local driver to take you from place to place, especially if your schedule is tight. With someone else doing the driving, you can make a quick call on the way to each interview, to introduce yourself and make sure the respondent is at home and expecting your arrival.

Once you arrive, take some pictures or video of the outside of the respondent's home and neighborhood, so you'll remember the setting in which each interview took place. During the interview, ask to take photos or video of the various rooms of the house, of family members participating in the interview, and, of course, of whatever actions or tasks you ask the respondent to perform. Not only will these visuals help you remember details for your analysis, they will be invaluable in communicating your insights to others on the marketing team.

To supplement or replace an in-home visit, you can accompany consumers on a shopping trip, observing what they do and asking relevant questions to help you understand the actions that you observe. You can also arrange for visits to your target audience's workplace, if your product is relevant to this setting, or go along on a family outing, a picnic, or some other consumption situation that will provide better understanding.

This type of visit is qualitative and mostly for background, so it is not necessary to conduct a large number of such sessions to gain value. Unless you need to include a number of different demographic sub-groups or look at regional differences, seven to ten home visits should provide all the immersion you need to better understand your category and your consumers.

The differences between in-home qualitative interviews and formal **ethnography** is in the amount of time spent with each respondent, the level of detail you explore and capture, and the scope of the analysis you conduct on the data. Ethnography is a method of observation used by anthropologists to describe a group or culture, usually after intense periods of observation and interaction with selected subjects thought to be typical of the group. In ethnography for marketing purposes, the researcher may make several visits to the same subject households, or may interact with a broader social unit that includes the main subject's family, friends, and neighbors.

One ethnographic study, for example, studied cancer patients and their support systems. During the course of several months, the researchers met with the study subjects in their homes, accompanied them on doctor visits and other treatment sessions, met separately with care providers, close friends and relatives, joined in celebrations held to mark occasions such as the end of chemotherapy, and otherwise participated in their subjects' lives. Results of this study were used to develop support materials and means of communication with patients and their families, once the research identified the points at which treatment information is needed and how it is sought.

To do it well, this kind of in-depth study represents a major commitment of time and resources and requires considerable training. For most non-anthropologists, it's probably better to get your insights from occasional in-home visits, and hire professionals when a full-blown ethnography is appropriate.

Use Syndicated Services to Understand Lifestyles and Values

Another way to learn about consumer lifestyles, values, and the marketplace environment for your product is to subscribe to syndicated research studies to provide background and context.

The Yankelovich Monitor,™ for example, has been tracking changes in social trends and consumer behaviors since 1971. Each year, results of a new Monitor survey of 2,500 U.S. adults aged 16 and over are analyzed in the context of this long history, allowing for identification of changes in consumer attitudes, opinions, beliefs, and values across a wide range of issues and population segments. Details of the research are available only to subscribers, but overall findings are widely reported in the media, and this information alone can add to your understanding of the consumer environment.

Yankelovich Partners also conducts Monitor studies on children, teens, and ethnic minorities. Other research firms conduct their own continuous tracking studies of opinions and trends. Trade associations, media firms, and other industry sources may have such information available to members, advertisers, or customers. Seek out these sources for your particular industry and become as familiar as possible with the information they provide. Look for trend articles in magazines and newspapers. Pay attention to recurring themes in current movies, books, and television programming. Tune in to the cultural environment around you, rather than trying to block it out. By starting with an understanding of the big picture, you will gain better insight from your own research by seeing your findings in a broader context.

Other syndicated or specialized services can give you an understanding of the living patterns, consumption habits, and core values of your current customers, prospects, or consumers who may represent targets of opportunity for the growth of your business. Each year Simmons Market Research Bureau (SMRB) and Mediamark Research Inc. (MRI) conduct major studies of consumer behavior. Both studies are similar in that they ask large national samples of consumers detailed questions about the media they consume, the products they buy, and the activities in which they participate.

Each study results in a huge database of information that can provide subscribers with in-depth profiles of any target group defined on the basis of media exposure, product use, or other questions included in the survey. Once you've defined a group of interest, you can run a report that shows how your target group compares with all U.S. households on other variables of interest, including usage of other product categories and brands, participation in a large battery of lifestyle activities, measures of attitudes and opinions, and self-described personality traits. Analysis of these relationships can tell you whether beer drinkers are more likely to play baseball or go bowling, or whether families who visit theme parks are more or less likely than non-visitors to also take their children to museums or zoos. The relationships revealed in these reports can be a rich source of insight and inspiration.

Geodemographic segmentation is a method that takes the detailed information gathered on a block-by-block basis in the U.S. Census, combines it with data from MRI or SMRB studies, and creates a scheme for categorizing individual neighborhoods based on the characteristics and lifestyles of the people who live there. These segments, or clusters, are typically given names that encapsulate key characteristics of the households they include, and can be used to identify similar types of households scattered throughout the country.

PRIZM,™ a product of Claritas, Inc., is the original and best-known geodemographic system, but other commercial providers use the same information to come up with similar segments. Geodemographic clustering systems are also available in some other countries where adequate census information is available for analysis. Most systems categorize ZIP codes, census tracts and block groups, which are the smallest unit of geography for which census information is reported.

Geodemographic clustering is frequently used to identify households that match the characteristics of a pre-defined target audience in a direct-marketing program or retail site location, but it can also provide an interesting portrait of consumers who are most likely to use a particular product category or service, and is invaluable in profiling the characteristics of customers in a database that includes individual addresses.

If you are engaged in database marketing, geodemographic profiling of your customers can be an easy first step in learning about their lifestyles, interests, and buying habits. Match each address in your database to its appropriate cluster, and then look at which clusters include large concentrations of your customers. If you have purchasing data on your file, relating the cluster code to amount spent, purchase frequency or other behaviors might lead to new ideas or insights that can translate into better marketing or opportunities for growth.

If you don't have a customer database, geodemographic clustering can still be useful, especially if you can identify the clusters that are more likely than average to use the product category you are interested in or who engage in the activity you are trying to promote. By looking at cluster descriptions and detailed information about the other behaviors of these households, you will gain a better understanding of the household composition, economic level, interests and values of the consumers you are trying to reach.

Values segmentation is another way to look at the attitudes, motivations, and lifestyles of groups within the general population that may be more or less likely to use or want your products or services. The original values segmentation system, VALS,™ was developed in the 1970s to look at consumer values and lifestyles, and was initially based on Maslow's Hierarchy of Values. More recently, the system has been modified to emphasize classification on the basis of enduring personality characteristics, rather than socially influenced values that may change over time. VALS is a product of SRI Consulting Business Intelligence.

The VALS system identifies three primary motivations that drive an individual's choices and activities: ideals, achievement, or self-expression. It combines these motivations with personality traits such as energy, self-confidence, impulsiveness, and vanity, taken in conjunction with basic demographic characteristics like age and income, to assign each person to one of the segments. Each segment has a different profile, based on what motivations are dominant and which personality traits have the strongest influence on behavior. A questionnaire that can be used to assign individuals to their dominant VALS segment is made available for use in custom research studies, and has also been included in syndicated surveys such as Mediamark Research Inc.'s annual *Survey of American Consumers*.

Knowing which VALS segments are predominant in your target group can add personality and dimension to your audience profile.

Use Custom Research to Get More Specific

Sometimes, you will have a clear enough picture of your target audience's lifestyle and motivations from your background analysis of secondary sources, but other times, you'll need to do more specific research to get at issues that are important to your understanding. Sometimes, the main objective of your research will be to learn about your target audience's attitudes, lifestyle, or motivations. On other occasions you can add questions or activities to research studies with some other purpose, to learn a little about your target as well as get their answers to your primary research questions.

For instance, if you are doing a series of focus groups to learn more about basic habits and practices in a product category that is new to you, add a homework assignment to give you better insight into how the product fits into the consumer's life, or devote a little time in the group for this exploration.

A good homework assignment that amounts to a sort of virtual in-home visit is to provide your respondents with inexpensive disposable cameras (or let them use their own, if they prefer) and have them prepare a **photo diary** of a typical day or a typical occasion for using the product you are interested in. Ask them to take eight to ten photos that will tell a story they can share with others in the group, that illustrate what it's like in their household on the specified occasion, whether it's the baby's first birthday, or barbeque time, or early morning, or time to take the dog for a walk. Make sure they get the cameras far enough in advance of the focus group to take the photos and get the film developed, or use digital cameras if time is an issue. The photo-illustrated stories will include more detail and reveal more insights than you'll get from respondents trying to recall their actions and thoughts on these occasions. Once again, the photos will be a valuable resource you can use to communicate the stories to the rest of your marketing team.

You can also use **collages** to get at lifestyles and interests as well as brand imagery and other metaphorical thinking. Ask consumers to create a collage that conveys their feelings and impressions about the topic, using clippings from magazines, scrap paper, their own drawings, or any other bits of material you or they might feel is relevant. You can have individual consumers create collages on their own at home, or you can use individual or group collage-building as an activity in a face-to-face interview. Just make sure the instructions are clear and that your respondents understand that you are looking for something that represents their impressions, not a literal depiction of the subject matter.

If you are using Collage to assess brand imagery, provide all your collage-builders with the same set of materials to work with, so you can see which pictures, words, and themes are consistently selected or left out. You can do this by giving each respondent a set of magazines from which to clip images to use in the collage, or you can pre-clip a large set of images yourself.

If you are more interested in learning how consumers feel about an experience or some aspect of their lives, it may be more productive to let consumers choose their own raw materials. This gives them the freedom to select any image or clipping that has meaning for them, and may uncover ideas or themes you had not even thought of.

In a project several years ago, groups of registered nurses were asked to create collages that represent the different aspects of life as a nurse, using clippings from magazines they found at home and brought with them to the interviews. Across ten sessions, in three different locations, the collages that emerged were remarkably similar. Each featured an image of a heart, usually placed quite near the center of the page, symbolizing, respondents said, the caring that nurses feel is the core value of their profession. Each collage also included at least one picture of hands, usually touching another person, as a representation of the direct, personal care the nurses said was their primary duty to patients. There were also babies shown in every collage, explained by respondents as representing the happiest, most joyful nursing experience—a shift in obstetrics.

Along with these positive images, each collage also contained depictions of the stresses and challenges of modern nursing. Every one showed at least one cold, metal tool, and at least one reference to electronics, robots, or automation, a reflection, nurses told us, of the increasingly mechanized and computerized medicine practiced today. Every collage also included references to stress, overload, and juggling, to illustrate the increased pressure nurses said they feel as their hospitals cut back on professional staff in an effort to control rising costs.

Some of these topics had been touched on during the question and answer portion of the interview, but some, especially some of the more positive associations, had not emerged until the collage-building exercise. Using collages in this case helped uncover the shared values of the profession, as well as the challenges of day-to-day nursing practice.

Picture drawing is another way of getting respondents to put your product into a broader context. Ask consumers to draw a picture representing some aspect of product use or some situation in their daily lives that you are investigating. For instance, if you're working on shampoo, ask respondents to draw pictures depicting "a bad hair day" and "a good hair day" and compare the two. If your respondents are like the ones who did this for me several years ago, you'll probably see lots of sunshine and smiles associated with good hair, and rain, lack of energy, wilted flowers, unhappiness, and big hats in the bad hair pictures.

Go a little further, and have respondents **tell a story**, in conjunction with picture drawing or separately. A bad hair day story might be full of unfortunate incidents like sleeping through the alarm, having trouble finding the right thing to wear, missing the bus, and other problems that have nothing to do with hair, but all seem to happen when you're not at your best.

Segmentation Research Identifies Attitudinal or Life-Stage Variations

In addition to adding lifestyle or context exploration to your qualitative research, you can conduct quantitative surveys designed to identify segments within your potential market, based on their attitudes and motivations, their perceived needs, or their life stages. These studies group consumers based on pre-determined dimensions such as their attitudes toward your product category, the motivations and needs they express in relation to your product, or the stage of life in which they find themselves. By segmenting your total market in these ways, you gain a better understanding of how you can market to the very personal needs of individual consumers by varying your message or your means of communication to more closely match the characteristics of each segment.

Attitude Segmentation is a means of dividing consumers, using various statistical clustering routines, to create groups of consumers who are as similar as possible to the others in the same group and as different as possible from those in other groups, based on their answers to questions in your survey. Questions used to create attitude segments will typically be agree-disagree statements that respondents answer on a five-, seven-, or ten-point scale that ranges from strong agreement to strong disagreement. To get the most insight, include two sets of these statements in your questionnaire. One set relates directly to product attributes and benefits, such as "I prefer a shampoo with a pleasant floral fragrance," or "I need a shampoo with a powerful cleaning agent to get my hair really clean." The second set of statements express personal preferences, feelings or motivations, such as "I just don't feel good if my hair needs washing," or "My hair makes me feel sexy." Participants respond to both sets of statements, as well as other questions that will be used to profile the segments on dimensions such as frequency and quantity of product use, usage and purchase patterns, brand preferences, and detailed demographics.

Usually, a study will use either the attribute-heavy product-based statements or the more motivational statements as the basis for segmentation, and then in analysis see how the segments derived from this clustering differ on all other questions in the study. Typically, you'll use the profile information to give catchy names to the segments, capturing the essence of each group's expectations or motivations with each short-hand label. You'll know your segmentation study is a success when you hear co-workers referring to the "Raven-Haired Beauties" or the "Tangle-Tamers" in ordinary conversation about your consumers.

Life-stage segmentation is another way to look at consumer needs and expectations, based on the major events and responsibilities of each person's current life, rather than fixed characteristics such as age or educational level. Life-stage theory says that people in similar stages of their lives have needs, concerns, and motivations in common, even when they may represent a mix of ages, educational levels, ethnicities or other characteristics. For some products, life-stage is almost certainly a crucial consideration. First-time parents of new babies, for example, probably share many needs, attitudes, and emotions, regardless of their ages or other characteristics. First-time home-buyers may have similar needs. Parents of teenagers certainly have much in common. Life-stage segmentation can be a useful way to isolate the factors that make your product appealing or necessary to consumers at that point in their lives.

On the other hand, sometimes other factors are more important, or must be taken into account in addition to life stage. Just imagine two new mothers—one a 17-year-old single mom who barely finished high school, leaves the baby with her mother while she works, and goes to community college, and the other a married, 35-year-old working professional with a live-in nanny, a supportive husband,

and a six-figure income. How you market diapers or baby food to these new mothers may depend on each one's personal characteristics as much as on her motherhood.

To get at the relative importance of life stage versus other factors, include plenty of questions about life-stage issues in your segmentation study, and analyze the findings to see if life stage, attitudes, or some combination do the best job of describing your ideal consumer targets.

Take Gender, Ethnicity, and Culture into Account

Because so much of the work done in search of consumer insights is qualitative and personal, cultural and gender-based differences among and between consumers and marketers can cause problems. Gender, ethnicity, and even the social norms that predominate in a particular region or community can lead consumers to express their thoughts and feelings in very different ways, even if the underlying intents and reactions are the same.

In some cultures, for example, it is considered impolite to express criticism, and a marketer not aware of this constraint can be misled by seemingly favorable comments that, on second analysis, are a polite way of avoiding conflict or evading an outright negative response. On the other hand, listening to a focus group of hypercritical New Yorkers comment on a new product concept can be torture for a marketer who sees a pet project being ripped to shreds, only to find out at the end of the group that almost every respondent is interested in buying the product when it becomes available.

Gender differences compound the problem. Although individuals do not always fit their gender pattern, in general, women express reactions and criticisms differently from the way men express the same ideas. There may also be a gender-based difference in the way consumers react to the person conducting the interview or presenting the new product concept. That doesn't mean that only women can interview women and men should only talk to men, but it does mean that your analysis of any consumer encounter should take into account the gender mix of respondents and interviewers as you interpret what is said and observed.

Race and ethnicity are other factors to consider. Opinions and reactions expressed in an ethnically mixed group may be different than when consumers feel they are "talking among themselves" with people of the same race or ethnicity. As with gender, the race and ethnicity of the interviewer or observer also may affect what is said and not said, and careful interpretation of both language and non-verbal response is important.

In addition to recognizing cultural differences in the meaning of what consumers say and do, it's also important to be aware of how differences in social norms and cultural experiences can create differences in how consumers think and feel. If your target audience includes different ethnic or cultural groups within the U.S., or if you are engaged in multinational marketing programs, it is essential that you become an expert in the cultural norms and expectations of the consumers you must influence. Learn as much as you can about the countries, neighborhoods or cultural groups you are trying to reach. Visit. Read books. Pay attention to the arts and crafts produced within these cultures. Listen to the music. Go to films and watch TV programs, even if reading subtitles is not your favorite form of entertainment. Reaching across cultural boundaries is not easy, but understanding the cultures and people you are trying to touch is an essential foundation for gaining insight.

NINE

Techniques for Understanding Imagery and Metaphor

CONSUMER RESPONSES to products, marketing messages, people, and other stimuli are often largely non-verbal, emotionally based, and "illogical." Most people can't easily describe or convey these reactions, yet marketers need consumers to put their non-verbal feelings and perceptions into words. We write strategies in words, and develop advertising in words, and present recommendations in words, even if the recommendation is to create an almost totally non-verbal marketing message. It's important to get the words right, as difficult as that may be, and sometimes, the best insight is finding a way to express what the consumer is feeling so that other members of the team can understand.

When you are trying to understand sensory response, imagery, and metaphor, straightforward questioning is rarely effective and can even obscure the response you are trying to explore. Consumers find it difficult to describe in words the sensory satisfaction they get from products, or the impressions or images they associate with people, places, or brand names. They don't readily talk about their emotional responses, and may not even recognize or recall some emotions they feel as consumers unless you find ways to intensify their consciousness or reactivate their memories. When most people try to put their feelings or impressions into words, they come up with logical

Some material in this chapter was originally included in Qualitative Research in the '90s: Issues, Approaches, New Technologies, an ARF Key Issues Workshop held June 18, 1996 in New York by the Advertising Research Foundation.

and rational statements that protect their dignity, enhance their self-perception and fit with their beliefs about what others expect of them. To really understand emotion-based responses, you need techniques that get around the rationalistic logic-monitor inside each of us and encourage expression of the truth you are trying to reveal.

Atmosphere and Surroundings Matter

When doing research on metaphor, sensation, and imagery, you need to create a physical and psychological environment that helps these deeper responses emerge. When you want to probe non-verbal feelings, choose the research location to help, not hinder, your efforts. Look for a relaxed, low-risk atmosphere that lets you connect with your subjects and create a playful, creative mood. Avoid questions that put respondents on the spot, or make them feel pressured to come up with a "meaningful" answer. Engage your respondents in the challenge of understanding and expressing reactions, feelings, and associations they have probably never consciously thought about before, and make this exploration an interesting way for them to learn something new about themselves.

In a qualitative setting, use these techniques in small group interviews, if possible. One-on-one, a respondent is more likely to feel threatened or stupid, and he may become non-responsive. In a larger group, some will struggle while one or two people will find the tasks easy and their ideas will tend to dominate. The ideal size seems to be from three to five people at a time, large enough to provide the respondents with safety in numbers, but small enough to allow for each person's individuality to emerge.

Think carefully about the way the interview room looks. Some research facilities have a more relaxed feeling than the typical boardroom-style focus group room. Look for couches, low tables, rugs, and pictures on the wall. If you're stuck in a traditional conference room, reduce the size of the table if you can, to reduce the distance between you and your respondents. Ask the facility to add some green plants or wall posters to reduce the starkness of the room. Make sure to serve refreshments, and put the drinks and snacks on the table within easy reach, so respondents can help themselves throughout the session.

From the very beginning, let respondents know you'll be asking them to do more than answer direct questions, and plan to use a variety of techniques to get at all aspects of the issue you are exploring. Describe the activities you'll be using as games or creativity exercises designed to help people think about a topic in new ways. Tell the group you're sure they'll think some of the things they will be doing are strange or silly, but ask them to go along with you and have fun. And be sure to stress that there are no right or wrong ways to complete the exercises you'll be asking them to do, so they can relax and express their true feelings.

Maintain a low-pressure atmosphere, but keep the pace moving along. If one technique doesn't work, don't dwell on it. That only makes respondents uncomfortable and may inhibit their responses to the next task. If the group finds an exercise really difficult, give them something easy to talk about before going on to another approach. If, on the other hand, they really get into a task, they'll be enthusiastic and want to move on to a new challenge fairly quickly, so don't slow them down with excessive probing. You'll find that once you've generated momentum, each new exercise builds on earlier ideas, and they'll go fairly quickly.

Choose the Right Techniques for Putting Feelings into Words

Qualitative researchers have been struggling with the question of how to probe emotions and sensations for years, and have developed many useful techniques to use in addition to, or as a substitute for, direct questioning. Sometimes, all these approaches are lumped under the general label of "projectives," but both this categorization and the label itself are misleading. Each technique has its own purpose and application, so one "projective" technique is not necessarily the equivalent of another, and many are not based on the psychological principle of projection at all.

A better name for these methods might be verbalization tools— techniques that use a variety of approaches to help stimulate verbal discussion of non-verbal emotions, perceptions, and sensations. Verbalization tools help consumers think and talk about their internal reactions but encourage non-linear responses that are more consistent with the nature of the reactions themselves. The most successful of these tools shifts the consumer's frame of reference on a topic, giving him or her a new perspective that can lead to surprising insights.

Anyone working in consumer insights needs to be familiar with a full array of verbalization tools. When planning an exploration of non-verbal reactions, think about which techniques most closely fit your topic and your objectives, and select several different approaches to make sure you explore from all angles.

Some of these exercises are primarily metaphorical—that is, they help respondents express their feelings and reactions toward one subject in terms of another, usually more concrete, idea. Others are more dependent on projection—the idea that people are more willing to express thoughts and feelings, especially deeply personal or potentially risky ones, when they can detach themselves from their reactions by attributing them to another person, or other people in general.

As a general guideline, rely more on metaphorical techniques when you are trying to understand sensory reactions or impressionistic perceptions, because these tools will help respondents express feelings they may have never before tried to put into words or explain to someone else. Use projective techniques when you are probing sensitive topics or want to encourage respondents to express negative reactions. Projectives help people express ideas they may find unpleasant to talk about or that are potentially damaging to their self-images or to the way they portray themselves to others.

These methods are most often used in unstructured qualitative interviews, but many can be adapted for inclusion in quantitative surveys as well. Some require advance planning and special materials, but most require nothing more than a good explanation of the task, sometimes accompanied by a sheet of paper or some colored markers. Plan ahead as much as you can, but don't be afraid to introduce one of these techniques spontaneously when the flow of an interview seems to call for it, or when you want to shake things up a little. As you use these techniques, you'll become more aware of the particular strengths of each exercise and you'll be able to pull the right one from your toolkit at any opportune moment.

To Start the Metaphorical Flow, Get Personal

One of the easiest techniques to use on the spur of the moment is **personification.** That's when you ask respondents to think about the qualities and characteristics of a brand, and then imagine that it transforms into a human being with those same traits. Give them a moment to get the image of their imaginary brand-person in mind, stressing that you want them to think about the brand itself, not the type of person who might use that brand in real life. Then ask questions that paint a picture of the person the respondent is imagining: Is it a man or a woman? What is his/her age? What does he or she look like? How tall? What kind of body—muscular, flabby, delicate, lanky? How is he or she dressed? What does this person do for a living? What does he or she do for fun? What's important in this person's life? What are his or her interests? Values? Hopes and dreams?

In general, it's best to start with very specific questions about the physical make-up of the imaginary person, to help your respondents get comfortable with the exercise. Then, to fill out the picture, dig a little deeper with questions about the person's interests, ambitions, values, and dreams. Be sure to include questions that relate to the brand and category you are exploring. If you're asking about beer, you probably want to know what Mr. Budweiser's favorite sport is, what he likes to do to relax, and maybe what kind of woman he's attracted to. And, of course, ask about more than one brand. It's by comparing Mr. Budweiser with Mr. Coors and Mr. Heineken that the real learning will take place.

If your individual brand personifications need spicing up, or if you're most interested in exploring the relationships among brands in a category, go beyond simply describing each person and put them into relevant **scenarios** where they interact with each other. With beer brands, you might ask about how each brand would behave at a party. Would Mr. Budweiser be the host, the center of attention, the wallflower, or the bore that everyone else tries to avoid? If the brands are household cleaning products, present them as roommates who have to share chores, and ask respondents to imagine what each one would contribute to that situation.

In one cleaning tool project that included a brand respondents considered an expensive convenience only good for touch-ups, they expressed their feelings by insisting that the brand-roommate wouldn't do any of the work, but would pay for a housekeeper and spend her time having fun. In another situation, teenagers imagined how several brands of soft drinks would behave in high school. They described Coca-Cola as the All-American captain of the football team who dates Diet Coke, the peppy cheerleader. Pepsi-Cola was the well-liked class clown, and 7-UP was the quiet girl with long blond hair who keeps mostly to herself and plays the flute in the orchestra.

A further elaboration is to **draw the person** represented by the brand. Stress that stick figures are fine, and ask respondents to do their best to depict the person they are imagining. Give them some prompts, such as asking them to show what kind of clothing the person would wear, what his hairstyle or headgear would be like, what he might be holding or carrying, what kind of setting or surroundings he would be most comfortable in, and even what his name might be. Adding a name can provide surprising dimensions. Whether respondents pick old-fashioned names like Ethel or Herman, trendy names like Madison or Joshua, or a solid, steady Mary or John, can tell you a lot about their perceptions of the brand.

You can use personification to get at negative aspects of the brand by asking respondents to put their imaginary person on the **psychiatrist's couch.** Ask them what problem this person might need help with, and what he or she might say in a session with a psychiatrist. Probe for what the psychiatrist might say in return, to help the person with that problem. Depending on brand perceptions, you might hear about excessive shyness (for an unknown or under-promoted brand), split personality (for a brand with multiple purposes or no strong single image), depression, hypochondria, or a variety of other psychological problems that reveal weaknesses in your brand or positioning. You'll also learn from the psychiatrist's response whether respondents see the problem as serious or minor, fixable or fatal, and you might even get some interesting suggestions on how to get the brand back on its feet.

If all else fails, and you are still probing for negatives, kill the person off and ask respondents to write his or her **obituary.** This exercise works well for consumer products and services, but it is especially revealing when used to diagnose organizational problems with employees, customers, board members, and other groups of "insiders" who may be reluctant to come out with direct statements of the company's weaknesses.

In the obituary exercise, be specific as to what respondents are to do. Ask them to write just a few sentences that could serve as an obituary for the person-brand you are most interested in. It may be helpful to list the information found in a typical obituary, and tell respondents to be sure to include something on each topic. Ask for the person's name and age, the cause of death, the person's major accomplishments in life, the one thing he or she will be most remembered for, who attended the funeral, and who are the heirs or survivors. In most cases, it's best to have respondents complete the exercise and collect the papers for review later, without making anyone read their obituaries aloud. If you want to share with the group, read selected passages yourself, without identifying the author, and ask for reactions.

When board members of a Chicago not-for-profit arts organization wrote obituaries a few years ago, two major themes emerged. One was the fear shared by many of the organization's leaders that the group's mission had become outdated and meaningless. They expressed this concern by referring to the deceased as a very old

woman who used to be famous, but had become a recluse, or as someone who had no mourners because she had outlived all her friends.
The obituaries also brought out the group's fears for the organization's major asset, a landmark building in a wealthy neighborhood,
worth several million dollars, with references to the real estate agents
and condominium developers who attended the funeral. Partly due to
the open discussions that this exercise made possible, the group undertook a renovation of both its building and its primary activities, to
move the organization solidly into the future.

If People Don't Work, Try Something Completely Different

Sometimes, especially when you are trying to learn more about perceptions of brand users, a celebrity spokesperson or other human
beings, it's best to stay away from the personification techniques and
try something completely different.

One useful technique that can be done on the spur of the moment
with almost any type of respondent is **shape-matching.** Draw four
shapes on a flip chart, or give respondents a sheet of paper with one
shape in each quadrant. Ask them to quickly pick the shape that they
most associate with whatever or whoever you are exploring. Then ask
for feedback about their choices—that is, what makes the shape they
picked the most appropriate choice.

FIGURE 9.1

Shape-Matching

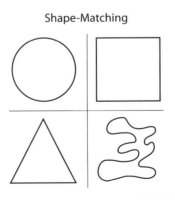

This technique works for two reasons. First, the shapes are so far removed from the reality of what you are trying to explore that matching a brand, a person, or a situation to these shapes forces the consumer to think about the topic in a different way. Explaining their choice calls for fresh language they may have never applied to this topic. Sometimes they'll even surprise themselves. Secondly, psychologists have found that shapes have universally recognized associations. Circles tend to make us think of wholeness, harmony, oneness, and love. Squares conjure up feelings of security, strength, solidity, and practicality. Triangles convey action, energy, movement, and exploration, while the squiggle evokes creativity, imagination, artistry, and vision.

This technique was used in 1996 to gain a better understanding of the two U.S. Presidential candidates, incumbent President Bill Clinton and former Senate Majority Leader Bob Dole. When asked to pick which shape reminded them in some way of each candidate, respondents were virtually unanimous. Bob Dole was always a Square, and Bill Clinton was universally recognized as a Squiggle.

The most interesting aspect of this exercise was the reasons people gave for their selections, and the relationship between the words they chose and their own political leanings. Everyone saw Bob Dole as a Square, but to his supporters, this reflected his solidity, his dependable support of traditional Republican values, his predictable conservatism. For those less committed to this candidate, his "squareness" reflected an out-dated view of the world and a rigidity that prevented him from dealing with the most pressing issues of the day. Bill Clinton, the Squiggle, was almost exactly the opposite. To supporters, the squiggle reflected Clinton's creativity, his ability to adapt to any situation, and his openness to new approaches and political compromises that commentators were beginning to call "the third way." They saw this flexibility as an advantage that would enable him to find solutions for whatever problems might come his way as president. Clinton-bashers, on the other hand, found the squiggle the perfect choice for other reasons. For them, the shape's flexibility and lack of definition reflected Clinton's "slippery" character, his willingness to cut corners or bend the rules of a situation, and the inability of his opponents to ever pin him down or set limits on his actions. Same candidates, different perspectives, and new insights as to how to describe each man, in both positive and negative messages.

Another on-the-fly exercise that can provide multiple perspectives on a brand image or personality is **analogies**. This technique also asks respondents to shift their frame of reference, using words and relationships from other categories to express their opinions and feelings. The task is simply to equate the brand or product in question to something else with similar characteristics.

Start by asking "If (brand) were a (something from a different category), which one would it be?" Choose categories that are removed from what you are studying, but may share some characteristics. Pick categories your respondents will be familiar with, but don't be afraid to go outside their traditional areas of interest. Categories that most people seem able to work with include cities or places, types of music, brands or types of cars, sports and leisure activities, animals or flowers. Use several categories to get a fully rounded picture of your brand image.

In analysis, look for common characteristics of the choices respondents make in each world to generate insights. For example, a brand that is described as a Ford, a daisy, a baseball, and a small town is probably seen as an ordinary, middle-of-the-road, perhaps slightly boring but acceptable choice. On the other hand, a Ford-dandelion-baseball-landfill has some serious problems, while a Mercedes-orchid-polo-Paris clearly has aspirational or luxury appeal, but may be far removed from respondents' personal experiences.

To get more deeply into imagery than individual analogies can go, ask respondents to **build-a-world** around their brand image. For instance, if you are exploring the differences in imagery conveyed by different brands of tea, ask them to describe a tea shop that would exclusively feature one brand, compared with a different tea shop that would use a different brand. Ask for descriptions of the place itself, the decor, the staff, the mood or feeling upon entering the place, the other items that might be on the menu, the customers who would frequent this shop and any other details you can think of.

Several years ago, an advertising agency for a major food company used build-a-world to learn more about the distinction consumers make between "pure" and "natural" as a descriptor for a fruit juice product. This became an issue when consumers repeatedly referred to their favorite juice as "pure and natural" and did not seem able to differentiate between the two descriptors. When probed directly, interpretation of the two words seemed to be circular—pure juice is natural, and natural juice is pure, and both are healthy and desirable—but it was not clear whether the words were really synonyms for each other, or if each represented a different aspect of the product.

To get at the distinction, we respondents were asked to imagine a new restaurant named "Pure" and another named "Natural," and describe in detail what these two restaurants would be like. This technique, unlike any tried earlier, broke through the apparent equivalence of the two terms and clearly illuminated what each word connotes.

The restaurant "Pure," respondents said, would be white and spare, with shiny tile floors and walls, cool fluorescent lighting, and a studied and scientific approach to food. This restaurant would use food free of any chemicals or additives, but mostly free of flavor as well, with lots of clear broth and cold raw dishes. The atmosphere would be efficient, not relaxed, and customers would be primarily health-driven, on special diets and very serious about the foods they consume.

"Natural," the restaurant down the street, would have a very different look, feel, and clientele. The food at "Natural" would also be additive-free and wholesome, but the emphasis would be on freshness, flavor, and enjoyment. The restaurant would be decorated with wood, soft colors, gingham, chintz and lots of flowers and plants. The atmosphere would be cozy and relaxed, and the customers would be casual people who care about high quality and come to eat good food with friends and family.

To use build-a-world, pick a construction project that fits your problem. As in the previous example, consumers seem readily able to imagine distinctly different restaurant worlds, but the technique is by no means limited to food and drink applications. To probe attitudes and imagery associated with typical fun-in-the-sun vacation destinations, you might ask consumers to describe spas called "California," "Florida" and "Arizona." You can even ask consumers to do some space traveling, and describe what they would see if they landed on a planet named after a brand. Comparing descriptions of Planet Lexus, Planet Cadillac, and Planet Volvo could well lead to new insights on the differences among upscale automobiles.

Picture Sorts Can Stimulate Response

Sometimes, it's best to give consumers some help in forming their ideas, by giving them visual aids such as sets of pictures or other types of sensory stimuli that help them express the feelings you are after. There are a number of different techniques that involve the use of a photo deck from which respondents choose photos most relevant to the question you pose.

Visual profiling is an excellent way to get at user imagery. With this technique, consumers sort through a large number of photos of people to identify the ones most likely to use each brand you are studying. There are two ways to have respondents complete this task. You can ask them to go through a deck of thirty to forty photos, separating them into two groups: those who would use a brand and those who would not. Or, they can be asked to sort into groups based on brand use, putting each picture next to the brand that person is most likely to use. The latter approach is more likely to differentiate among brands, while the former will create a profile that is, to some degree, based on perceptions of category users as a whole.

The success of visual profiling is highly dependent on the range of photos you include in the deck, especially if you are trying to get at differences in perceptions of brands, rather than category use overall. Photos cut from magazines or selected from clip art archives are fine, but choose carefully. Ideally, the photos will include some cues as to the person's personality or lifestyl, from his physical appearance, clothing, background setting, or all of these elements. Choose pictures that depict a wide range of individuals, including photos of both men and women if your product category appeals to both. Always include a range of ages, ethnicities, and economic levels for each gender.

Pick photos of people who might be users of the product category, even though they may not be the tightly defined market segment that is your primary target audience. Make sure the intended target is represented, but include other age groups, personality types, or economic levels so you'll know whether consumers have a different view of who your product attracts. Don't include children or teens if your category is an alcoholic beverage, and leave out frail-looking senior citizens if you're researching brand images for mountain bikes or cross-country skis, but don't limit yourself to only the most obvious choices.

While it might seem appropriate to keep the portraits fairly consistent, doing so will defeat the purpose of the exercise. Above all, avoid head shot portraits with blank backgrounds and few cues to personality. Your respondents will start to feel as if they are looking at a high school yearbook, and there will not be enough difference in the photos to give you much information.

It's usually a good idea to include a few pictures of edgier or odd-looking people, along with more average-looking individuals. Avoid stacking the deck with gorgeous model types, although do include some photos of very attractive people, to see if one of the brands has an aspirational quality evidenced by a disproportionate association with the best-looking or most affluent-looking types.

When you interpret the results of your sort, try to first take in the impression left by all the photos for one brand as a group, rather than searching for the meaning in each individual choice. That's the way you'll see if one brand is considerably older or younger than another, or whether one tends to be associated with white-collar people while the other is seen as more for blue-collar types. By looking at each brand's group as a whole, you'll be able to see if there is an ethnic or gender skew, or, as often happens, all the "nerds" are associated with the brand that has the weakest or least-appealing brand image.

If you're doing this exercise in a group, it can be interesting to post the photos associated with each brand where the group can see them, and ask respondents for their own interpretations. Wait to do this until you've categorized each brand, however, or the results for one brand may influence the categorization for the next.

Although you should not mix recognizable celebrities with anonymous people in your photo deck, you can do the same exercise using all celebrity photos, which may be easier to find in magazines or in photo archives. Again, just be sure to include a wide range of people, personality types, genders, ages, and ethnic groups, the same as if you were using anonymous photos. Then ask respondents to assume that the celebrity, or a character he or she might play, would use the product category you are studying, and ask them to decide which brand each person would be more likely to use. This exercise is harder to do for ordinary household products, because consumers have a hard time imagining celebrities doing mundane tasks, but it works quite well for image-related or status-heavy categories like fashion, cosmetics, personal care products, beverages, and the like.

A similar exercise that gets at **metaphorical association** rather than user imagery is conducted the same way as visual profiling, but uses a different deck of photos. For this exercise, you'll need photos of objects or scenes that evoke strong emotional responses or moods. Ask respondents to quickly select the photos they associate with the brand or subject you are studying in some way. First impressions produce better results than studied thought. From a deck of fifteen or twenty choices, you might ask respondents to pick the two or three most relevant photos, and then carefully probe as to what made them select each one. In this exercise, it is especially important that your questioning be very neutral. Do not assume that, for instance, a photo of a heavy piece of construction machinery connotes power and force. The consumer might have picked it to express a feeling of coldness and inhumanity, or some other idea entirely.

A variation of this technique is to use a deck of pictures representing different objects in the same category such as animals, pieces of furniture, flowers and plants, tools, fruits and vegetables, sports equipment, or almost anything else where a single category of things includes sufficient variety to be useful. Pick a type of object that is unrelated to your topic, but that may have some relevance to the issues you expect to be important.

In this exercise, a respondent might associate one credit card with a Swiss Army knife and another with a padlock. Probing these associations could reveal a desire to have one card that is accepted everywhere to use for everyday spending, and another that can be "locked away" for use in emergencies or reserved for just one kind of purchase, such as school tuition or vacation travel.

Another exercise you can do with a deck of emotional or metaphorical pictures is **visual storytelling.** This technique allows you to probe the emotional aspects of complex decision-making processes, without asking direct questions about feelings and emotions. It's a way to look for the emotions that come and go during a multi-step process by giving consumers a visual language for recalling and talking about their feelings rather than their behavior or their rational decision-making.

In visual storytelling, use a set of emotion-rich or evocative pictures, and develop a series of stages or decision-points in the process you are studying. For example, if you are interested in new-car purchasing, you might outline a process that starts with the consumer's realization that it's time to get a new car, working through information-gathering and shopping behavior, the final selection, the sales negotiation, signing the contract, driving off in the new car, and so on, for as far into the pre- and post-purchase cycle that interests you.

For each decision-point you specify, ask respondents to select a picture that in some way represents what they were thinking or feeling at that moment. Once they've made their matches, they talk about why each picture fits their situation, probing for the emotions that underlie the photos they selected.

For this technique to be most successful, the pictures must be far removed from the reality of the process or situation you are studying. In the new-car study, for example, the photo deck did not include any pictures of traffic or cars on the road. Instead, there were photos of a bolt of lightning, a prison chain gang, an airplane taking off, a befuddled student writing confusing equations on a blackboard, a vicious dog (which some respondents said represented the car sales-man), and other depictions of moods or feelings, rather than recog-nizable people or situations. A credit card study used many of the same photos, as well as a deep-sea diver (in over his head, some respondents said), a door opening to a limitless horizon, a swimming class of babies floating in a pool, a fat cat chewing on a hundred dol-lar bill, and a stylized drawing of well-dressed professionals climbing the ladder of success. In each study, the actual pictures a respondent selected were less important than the reasons given for each choice. In discussing what was meaningful about the photo, consumers revealed aspects of their true feelings that did not emerge in any other part of the study.

To Probe Sensory Reactions, Use Sensory Stimuli

When you are trying to explore issues like "good" taste or the feel-ing of "refreshment," it is especially difficult to get consumers to artic-ulate their feelings and perceptions. In these situations, it can be helpful to use stimuli that force the consumer to use senses other than sight to find the metaphorical connections that produce insight.

For example, you might explore "refreshment" by asking respon-dents to smell a number of different fragrances—both pleasant and unpleasant—and identify the ones they find "refreshing" or "not refreshing." Then ask what it is about the odors that make them refreshing or not, and you are on your way to a definition of this very difficult-to-define concept.

In the same study, you could relate the sense of touch to refresh-ment by giving consumers a set of fabric swatches, hidden from view in a paper bag, and ask them to select the one that represents "refreshment" better than the others. Again, ask why, and more dimensions of refreshment will be revealed.

You can also use auditory stimuli—different sounds—to explore similar concepts. Imagine the sounds that would be associated with "trust" or "safety" and think of how different they would be from sounds that say "refreshment" or "excitement."

Tastes work as well, although it is probably best to stay away from taste stimuli if you are studying a food product in order to avoid overly literal selections. To use taste as a stimulus, you could use different flavors of hard candy, or blindfold your respondents and give them bite-sized servings of foods like cheese, peanut butter, fruits, or similar items. For safety's sake, just be sure to ask ahead of time if your respondents have any allergies that might prevent them from tasting certain foods.

TEN

Techniques for Understanding Features and Benefits

ANY PRODUCT, service or idea that becomes the object of a marketing effort has concrete features and benefits that fill both rational and emotional needs for the consumer. Learning what the product has to offer, and how consumers think and feel about its features and benefits leads to better insights into how best to reach the target audience and motivate them to buy.

Before doing any kind of marketing, it's important to know your product inside and out, both from the perspective of the insiders trying to sell it and from the point of view of the consumer you want to influence. Before you begin marketing, take an objective look at what you are trying to sell and how it meets the needs of your target audience. Make sure you continue to monitor both the internal aspects of the product and consumer perceptions of it as your marketing program continues.

Learning about the Product from the Inside

Begin by taking an in-depth look at the objective facts about your product. Ask yourself honestly, what does it do, really? Don't be satisfied with what previous marketing claims have been. Talk to the product designers or inventors, the engineers or chemists who put it together, and ask them to give you an objective, fact-based description of the product's functions and performance.

At the same time, find out how your product compares with competitors or substitutes in terms of appearance, formulas, physical characteristics and performance measures, and any other dimensions you can think of. Make sure everyone involved in this process provides an honest, objective assessment. If your product really does not measure up to the competition in some way, you need to know about it. If it is truly superior, you need to know in exactly what way, and how much better it really is, and how that makes a difference to the consumer.

A newcomer to a company marketing premium-priced herbs and spices asked, "How can we charge so much more than other brands?" and learned more than she (or consumers) may want to know about purity and contamination in lower-priced, lower-quality spices. She also learned that when consumers use her company's premium-priced, purer and fresher spices, they should adjust their recipes to use less, so the spice does not overpower the dish. Will this understanding lead to better insights in the future? It's hard to say. It is likely, however, that knowing about her product's higher concentration of pure spice and the flavor it imparts will influence her future market exploration.

Whether your product is a line of premium spices, or the newest whizz-bang mobile phone, or an old, established household cleaning liquid, learn how your quality control system works. Watch the testing process if you can. Learn what causes a product or batch to be rejected, and how many defective products are found and removed from distribution. Find out what happens to product that falls below quality control standards, and if possible, how your company's quality control operation compares with the systems used by your competitors.

Extend your investigation beyond the R&D lab or the manufacturing floor and learn everything you can about the distribution channels that get your product to the end consumer. Look at how your products are shipped, what kind of packaging protects them, and what issues or problems must be dealt with in transferring product from the manufacturer to the consumer. Sometimes, this exploration can identify features that become important elements of the brand positioning or marketing program, such as the constantly refrigerated distribution system used to keep Coors Beer cool and fresh from brewery to end-purchaser.

If you are marketing a service, look at every aspect of how the service is delivered. Examine the intended process—the "ideal" of what the consumer should be getting. Investigate the rationale behind the prescribed methods for handling each step of the service delivery. Learn how to recognize excellent performance and to distinguish it from an effort that is "just okay." Investigate everything that can go wrong, and learn how front-line service providers deal with unexpected problems or recover from mistakes. Look at the training the customer-contact people receive, how they are monitored, and what aspects of their performance are rewarded. You won't be successful promoting your company's commitment to giving each customer personalized attention if your telephone support staff is evaluated only on the number of calls they handle per hour, or how quickly they get each caller off the phone.

If you are involved in cause marketing, or any other marketing of ideas, think about the cause you are trying to promote. Look at the message you are trying to get across and the counter arguments posed by opponents or by others with a different perspective on the issue. Consider these ideas as objectively as you can, and try to find the merit in the other side's case, if for no other reason than to gain a better understanding of your adversary. Look at the media you and others are using to convey your messages—not just the actual communications channels you use, but also your organization's spokesperson or leadership, the outsiders who support or advocate your position, and any other stakeholders, proponents, or opponents who are engaged in the debate. Look at the issue in the broadest way possible before focusing in on your own goals and messages.

Whether you are marketing a product, a service, or an idea, look closely at the way your product is presented and sold to the end consumer. Talk with people in your direct sales force and find out what they think and feel about the product. Learn how they present features and benefits to their customers and prospects. Ask them what they find to be the most compelling aspects of the product. Find out what obstacles they encounter when trying to make a sale. Look for ways your marketing program can support their efforts, and how their experience can lead to your own new insights.

Spend some time at the retail setting, and learn as much as you can from the workers who have direct contact with the end purchaser. Talk with them about what their customers are looking for, what questions people ask, what complaints they raise, and what seems to either promote or inhibit the final purchase. These sales people may not know everything about the consumer that you can learn from systematic research and your own contacts, but their impressions and beliefs are an important part of the environmental mix that your marketing efforts have to work within.

As part of your retail research, look at how the product is displayed, what kind of impression it makes on the shelf or on the showroom floor, and how consumers interact with it prior to buying. Do shoppers pick up the package, read labels, touch the product and compare competitive brands? Do they spend as little time as possible making a decision? Do they look at the product display and immediately seek out help from a salesperson? Knowing how potential buyers approach the in-store task of choosing and buying your product is an important part of your background understanding.

Researching Consumer Perspectives on Product Features and Benefits

Once you've learned everything you can about your product from the internal perspective of your organization, it's time to look at your product from the outside and take steps to discover how consumers think and feel about what you have to offer.

When you start to research product-specific features and benefits, you'll be dealing mostly with the more cognitive, rational side of the brain. Product features are facts that potential consumers first need to learn about first so they can decide for themselves what benefits they deliver. Much of consumer activity related to features and benefits, and starts with a thinking process, rather than with emotions.

End benefits may well be emotional, or perceived more through sensation or feeling rather than through a logical thought process, but in general, features and benefits start on the thinking side of the spectrum.

Begin by Finding Out How Consumers Organize Their Perceptions

One of the first things you must understand about your category and brand is how consumers structure their thoughts about these products. Making groups and putting individual objects into categories is one of the ways we human beings learn at an early age to make sense of our surroundings. As we grow up and become consumers and buyers, we extend this practice into the marketplace, to help make sense of the enormous array of possibilities presented to us.

One of the best ways to understand how consumers structure a product category is with **perceptual mapping.** In a common approach to perceptual mapping, consumers complete a questionnaire that asks them to rate a wide range of choices in a category on a long list of attributes. Other statistical methods start with questionnaires that ask consumers to indicate the degree of similarity between pairs of brands overall and on individual attributes, but direct rating of attributes is a more straightforward task that may be easier for consumers to complete.

The attributes chosen for inclusion in the study represent the full range of ways in which consumers differentiate, or could differentiate, within the category. In a beverage study, the attributes might include taste factors such as level of sweetness, flavor, freshness, or other relevant descriptors, along with ideas like ability to quench thirst, calorie content, nutritional value, appropriateness for various consumption occasions, and so on. The choices consumers are asked to rate might be the competing brands within a tightly defined category, such as Coke, Pepsi, Mountain Dew, and Sprite, or could present alternative product choices that may fill the same or similar needs, for example, carbonated soft drink, bottled water, orange juice, iced tea, coffee, and milk.

Once consumers have rated each of these choices on all of the attributes, a multidimensional statistical routine determines which attributes or dimensions are most important in differentiating among the choices. Starting with the most important attribute, analysts use a statistical formula to select additional dimensions that add differentiation without duplicating the distinction made by the attributes already identified. In statistical terms, new attributes are added to the analysis only if they are uncorrelated with previously selected variables.

These attributes are typically visualized in a two-dimensional diagram as arrows pointing outward from a center meeting point. The length of the arrow shows how strongly that factor distinguishes one brand from another, while the direction of the arrow serves to mark a space on the map where that attribute is dominant.

Once the differentiating attributes have been identified, a score for each individual brand is calculated based on its ratings and the brands are placed on the map. Brands are placed closer to competitors they are similar to and into the space determined by their strongest attributes. The end result is a visual depiction of how consumers think about a category in terms of the product features and benefits they use to differentiate their choices, and their evaluation of each choice on those attributes.

You can do a similar kind of perceptual mapping in qualitative research by conducting a **brand** or **product sort** as part of a focus group discussion or individual in-depth interviews. This is a three-step process that helps identify the factors that distinguish among brands and places brands on a map representing the most important differentiating factors.

To start, ask your respondents to name as many brands or competitive options in your category as they can, whether they have used these brands or not. As they mention brands, record each name on a separate index card.

Once consumers have named the brands they know, and you have added any relevant brands they did not mention, you have the set of brands to be mapped.

Working with the whole set of brands, have respondents create groups, putting similar products in the same group, and making each group as different as possible.

An alternative approach is to use actual products, instead of writing brand names on index cards. This method introduces the visual and verbal cues present on packaging and may be a more appropriate way to position a new or unfamiliar brand within a category of better-known competitors.

Once all brands have been sorted, ask what the brands in each group have in common and how each group is different from the other groups created. The discussion of the similarities and differences between groups identifies the dimensions consumers use to organize or segment the product category. Across several individual interviews or several focus groups, you will start to see the same basic groups emerge and the same characteristics used to describe them, even if placement of some brands is inconsistent. You may also see some variation in the number of categories that emerge, with some consumers creating one large group that others divide into two or three different categories. In the end, your goal is to identify the most important characteristics, which then become the axes for your brand map.

For example, in a study of bottled salad dressing, one of the primary dimensions respondents use to differentiate among products is likely to be fat content or number of calories per serving. In the brand sort, you are likely to have some groups of "full fat" or "high calorie" products, some with lower fat content, and some with no fat at all. Another dimension may be whether the product is shelf-stable or is sold from the refrigerator case. Another may be a distinction between "everyday" and "special occasion" flavors or brands. In your analysis, you'll have to decide which of these differentiating characteristics are most relevant to your situation, and what insights you gain from the way consumers sorted the brands you included.

Of course, if the distinction between "diet" and "regular" brands seems obvious, and you are really only interested in how consumers think and feel about reduced calorie or reduced fat dressings, those types should be the only ones included in your brand sort. If you only care about refrigerated dressings, only use those. Working within the more restricted brand set will force consumers to think about less obvious differentiators and may lead to a better understanding of your brand's position versus its true competitors.

A refinement of this technique is to ask the group to discuss the most important differentiating factors in a category before conducting the brand sort, and then ask them to arrange the brands according to their perceptions of each brand on these key factors. This approach is most effective when the key differentiating factors are relatively few and have been well-documented in other research. You can use a one-dimensional scale and have consumers sort brands based on how much or how little of a single attribute each brand possesses, or you can give them a two-dimensional grid that makes them assess the relationship of two attributes. Either of these approaches is useful in new product development, where you can have consumers place new concepts on the appropriate scale, based on lists of features, package designs or positioning statements.

Brand sorts can be used to gain deeper insight into the results of quantitative perceptual mapping research, to guide development of questions for use in quantitative studies, or to gain a qualitative perspective on the way target market segments structure the competitive set of brands they have to choose from.

You can also use sorting with intangibles to gain a better understanding of how consumers think about a particular issue or a specific aspect of their lives. For example, I used this technique in several group interviews to map how young adults think about their range of leisure-time activities. After asking the group to generate a long list of ways they spend or could spend their leisure time, respondents placed the activities into categories based on any dimensions that were meaningful to them.

The first dimension that emerged was the difference between "at home" and "away from home" activities. Typical at-home leisure time is spent reading, watching TV or surfing the Internet. "Away" activities can include either solitary pursuits such as a walk in the park, shopping, or working out at the gym, or "things you do with friends" such as going to bars, clubs, restaurants, the movies, or museums, which are things that can be done any time, on the group's own schedule. In contrast were away-from-home activities that require sticking to a particular schedule, such as going to a concert or theater performance, attending a sporting event, or taking a workshop or class. This discussion helped local performing arts groups understand where their particular offerings fit into their potential audience's overall array of leisure options, and to identify the alternative activities they compete with most closely.

Assess the Value Consumers Place on Individual Features

If your initial work shows that decisions in your category are made on the basis of concrete and distinct attributes, rather than on some generally perceived image or feeling, you may want more information on how specific features and benefits influence choice. Unfortunately, simply asking consumers to rate the importance of individual product attributes usually results in high ratings for most items and little discrimination that can guide decision-making. As consumers, most people want it all, until they are faced with purchase situations that force them to make hard choices between desirable features.

Conjoint analysis, also know as trade-off research, can be a big help in finding out what really matters to your customers and which features and benefits they are willing to give up if necessary to get some other feature they desire more.

Conjoint analysis is based on the economic model that says consumers make rational assessments of the value of individual product features and choose the product that gives them the combination of variables with the highest utility for their needs. In a category where there are few objective differences among brands and consumers make decisions based on image and gut feelings, conjoint analysis will not provide much useful information. But, if your category is feature-driven, this technique can shed light on how individual consumers or segments within the total market weigh each attribute in their deci-sion-making. Computers, mobile phones, insurance, cruise lines, sports equipment, airline flights, restaurants, checking accounts and Internet service providers are only a handful of the types of products and ser-vices that might be good topics for conjoint analysis.

In a conjoint study, you begin by identifying key attributes and the "levels" of each attribute that reflect the range of choices in the cat-egory. You can use perceptual mapping or qualitative brand sorts to identify attributes; you can ask consumers what they see as the major differences between brands; or you can draw on your general knowl-edge of the category to decide what attributes are relevant.

Typically, one study will include three to five major attributes, each tested at three to five levels. Attributes like price or size can be expressed as numeric values, with relative descriptors such as small, medium, and large, or as levels above, at or below average for the category. Non-continuous variables need clear descriptors of the alter-natives. For instance, if you were measuring the importance of food service on airline flights, your alternatives might be "no food," "pret-zels or nuts," "a cold snack," or "a hot meal."

Once you've identified attributes and levels to be tested, you con-duct a survey presenting combinations of the attributes to consumers, who indicate on a scale their likelihood of choosing each combina-tion. Generally, all combinations of the attribute levels will be pre-sented in the study, although some methods allow subsets of the combinations to be selected for individual respondents, either on a random basis or on the basis of what the consumer rates as his or her most important decision-making criteria.

An alternative method is to ask respondents to choose from a set of products representing different packages of variables that cover the full range of options you are testing. This method more closely sim-ulates the decision-making consumers go through in the marketplace, where, for example, they may decide to trade off their preferred level of battery life on a laptop computer in order to get a lighter weight model or reduce the price they have to pay. If you're using the preference method, always allow consumers to "walk away" from the choices before them by indicating they would not choose any of the combinations you present, just as they might decide not to buy when they are unable to find the combination of features they want in the products offered for sale.

With either approach, statistical analysis is used to calculate "utilities" for the individual attributes. The numeric values of these utilities have no intrinsic meaning, but their relative sizes indicate how much each factor influences choice. It's possible to use these utilities to predict whether consumers will react favorably to a new product with a combination of attributes different from current competitors, or to segment consumers into groups based on the importance they place on individual attributes.

You can also use this technique to predict profitability, by assigning costs to each level of an attribute and using consumer preference to predict the relative sales that would occur under each combination of features. An example of this approach is how Dunkin' Donuts developed its new concept store, as described in Chapter 4.

Get to Core Benefits and Values

Sometimes, just knowing which features consumers want most is enough. If weight is more important than battery life in laptop computers, it's relatively easy to decide which feature to highlight in advertising, point of sale materials, and public relations efforts. However, many purchasing decisions are based on a combination of product features, the immediate benefits they provide, and higher-order benefits that tap into the individual consumer's core values. For these situations, you need techniques that allow you to dig deeper into the meaning of individual benefits and follow the trail to the value that provides the consumer's primary motivation.

One way to understand what role a product plays in the consumer's life, and what benefits it provides is to remove it and see what happens. In a **deprivation study,** regular consumers of a product agree to do without it for a specified period of time, keeping track of their thoughts and feelings during the deprivation period as well as recording what substitutes they find and how satisfactory these replacement products are. In his book, *Truth, Lies and Advertising,* Goodby, Silverstein & Partners Account Planner Jon Steel recounts how deprivation focus groups contributed to the development of the "Got Milk?" campaign developed by his agency for the California Fluid Milk Processors Advisory Board. After agreeing to go without milk for a week, focus group participants described how they felt when they realized their deprivation pledge meant they would be unable to enjoy a morning latte or that the chocolate chip cookies purchased as comfort food after a hard day were not the same without a cold glass of milk. The ad campaign taps into the emotion of these "no milk" moments by humorously depicting how running out of milk can ruin the enjoyment of other foods.

Deprivation studies are especially effective at uncovering the underlying benefits of products, like milk, that consumers use habitually, but often without consciously thinking about their value or importance. Imagine asking devoted Starbucks customers to go without coffee for a week, or taking mobile phones away from high-volume users for even a couple of days. The experience is almost certain to be traumatic for many, and learning how consumers deal with the deprivation could spark new insights into what may seem like a stagnant commodity category.

The opposite of deprivation is a **glut study**, in which consumers are provided with many times more product than they normally consume, and are asked to think of new or different ways to use it up. This technique is a good way to discover possible new uses for an established product, or to gain a better understanding of what needs the product satisfies and what even endless quantities of it can't provide.

Another way to understand features and benefits is to use **laddering**, an interviewing method that probes how basic product attributes deliver functional benefits leading to satisfaction of higher-level needs that address the consumer's core values.

Laddering is based on the idea that product attributes—both physical characteristics and less tangible features like value pricing or reputation for quality—provide direct functional benefits that consumers expect and can readily describe, but that those benefits link to higher-order benefits that ultimately tap into the values psychologists have identified as the basic motivators of human behavior. Values at the end of consumer ladders include ideas such as comfort, prosperity, pleasure, excitement, freedom, accomplishment, physical well-being, security, happiness, and self-esteem. The progression from attributes to benefits to values takes the consumer from surface-level rational thinking to deeper emotions and motivations.

A laddering interview is best done individually or in small groups of no more than two or three consumers at a time. It's not an appropriate technique for large focus groups or written surveys because these methods do not allow you to adequately probe each individual's responses. Conduct laddering interviews with category users only, since non-users will have little to contribute about the benefits your category delivers. You should also make sure users of the full range of brands are represented, since different brands may deliver different benefits to their users.

Begin a laddering interview by asking respondents to tell you what attributes they look for when selecting a product in the category. Use open-ended questions such as, "What helps you decide which brand to buy?" and "What makes one brand different from another?" As the respondent answers, a helpful technique is to jot down each attribute mentioned on an index card or separate piece of paper to use later in the interview.

The second step is to identify which attributes are important in the decision process. Using your index cards, ask the respondent to sort the attributes into three piles: very important, somewhat important, and not important in her choice of product or brand. To complete the interview, use the cards the respondent rated as most important to probe the benefits that the respondent derives from each of these product features.

Starting with a card chosen at random, ask the respondent to tell you about the benefit or result of that feature. Probe as deeply as you can, using as many different questions as you can think of. Some good probes are "What makes that a good thing?" or "When that happens, how does that affect things?" When appropriate, use probes to approach the issue from different sides, with questions like, "When does that occur?" or "What if the product didn't have this feature?" or "How does that make a difference?" As you probe, try to avoid repeating the same question, especially, "Why is that important?" or similar variations that can make respondents feel they're being grilled by a persistent five-year-old.

Keep going with your questions until you reach a core value, unless you sense that your questions are making the respondent too uncomfortable to go on. Usually, this won't happen, and you'll be pleased with how far your ladder reaches.

As you look at each chain of responses, organize the benefits into tiers. Start with the actual attribute, then move to the immediate benefit of that attribute. One attribute may have more than one immediate benefit. A low-fat food, for instance, may be lower in calories, but may also have no or low cholesterol. From each immediate benefit, track the indirect benefit, which respondents may express as the *result* of that benefit. For instance, lower calories may mean the product helps with weight control, while low cholesterol may mean prevention of heart disease.

Watch for multiple indirect benefits as well, in both interviewing and analysis. Lower calories may relate to weight control for some people, but may give others permission to eat more of a food they enjoy. These two ideas will lead to very different emotional benefits, the next step up the ladder. Better weight control may make consumers feel good about themselves, leading to more confidence, leading to the ultimate value of self-esteem. On the other hand, being able to eat more of a favorite food provides more immediate pleasure, which leads to greater enjoyment of life and the ultimate value of happiness.

ELEVEN

Putting It Together with Meaning

DOING GREAT RESEARCH and finding great insights will not lead to great marketing unless those insights can be communicated to the people responsible for developing the advertising, the promotions, the packaging and the retail environments that bring the consumer and the product together. Presenting the results of consumer insights research is as important as doing it because insights are only useful when they influence the way the whole corporate team interacts with the target audience.

Much of the difference between traditional research and consumer insights lies in the ways findings are analyzed, presented and put into use. In a traditional research setting, researchers present research results to the internal "clients" who requested the study, going through a detailed recounting of findings, and ending with conclusions and carefully couched recommendations that are taken as "suggestions" that the real decision-makers may or may not choose to follow.

In consumer insights, the emphasis is on getting to the conclusions—the insights—as quickly and as memorably as possible, and on working as partners with others in the organization to apply consumer insights to the business problem or opportunity. Instead of being used as a resource by others with decision-making responsibility, consumer insights specialists are as responsible as others in the organization for initiating research and for making sure that what the company knows about the consumer is used to guide all aspects of its operations.

To make the greatest impact on busy colleagues, practitioners of the consumer-insights approach have learned that presenting the detailed findings of complex research studies is not always the most effective and useful approach, even though findings and conclusions must be based on sound data. Instead, the consumer-insights specialist digests a study's findings, interprets their meaning, and presents the team with the essential knowledge team members need to move forward.

It's no accident that the consumer-insights approach has grown and developed along with the spread of PowerPoint presentations, computer graphics, and an emphasis on the multi-media communication of ideas. These are powerful tools that can help achieve the main goal of an insights-driven presentation, which is to turn abstract or conceptual findings into vivid, concrete realities that breathe life into our mental picture of the consumer.

Creative Briefs to Stimulate Creative Thinking

Perhaps because the emphasis on consumer insight originated in advertising agencies, an important means of communicating insight is the creative brief or briefing session. Originally aimed at ad agency "creatives" charged with the responsibility of actually developing advertising, **creative briefs** can be used more widely to convey meaningful consumer insights to all members of the marketing team who need this knowledge.

In advertising, the creative brief is the place to establish the goal for the advertising, to provide information on the audience the advertising is trying to reach, and to define the message the advertising is to convey. It guides the creative team to the most auspicious spot for reaching the consumer in a meaningful way. In other marketing contexts, creative briefs and the activity of briefing provide a summary of the most meaningful information about the market and the consumer, a synthesis of what has been learned through marketing research, observation, internal operations, conversation with distributors and retailers, and any other methods that have been used to study the issue in question.

Traditionally, advertisers have used the creative brief as a statement of the marketing or advertising strategy or a definition of the "rules" under which the brand will be advertised and marketed. Most companies that use creative briefs have a template for briefing—a form to be followed, specifying the project background, the objective, the target audience, the brand positioning, the message or primary brand benefit, the product features or other facts that support this benefit, the tone or mood of the communication, the media to be used, and a host of other details. Such a template can be a useful guide for putting together a brief, but filling in the blanks in a form does not make for the most useful briefing. A more meaningful approach is to tailor the format of the brief to the content, choosing the best method for presenting the ideas and insights you want to convey in any particular situation.

One thing most consumer-insights specialists try to avoid is the preparation of a long written document that is passed on to the marketing team without further discussion or interaction, whether it's a formal research report or a less traditional creative summary. Face-to-face communication of results is as important in consumer insights as face-to-face interaction with consumers. You may be able to do the job without it, but your chances of making real breakthroughs leading to great marketing are substantially less.

Some companies have built on the practice of in-person briefings by setting aside blocks of time for a particular team to discuss and apply the findings of a major research project. These half-day or full-day workshops may even be held off-site, to emphasize their importance and eliminate in-office distractions that interrupt the flow of discussion. The agenda for such a workshop includes the presentation of the research findings, but goes beyond that step to include brainstorming on how the research sheds light on a specific business problem. Such a meeting is not considered successful unless the team leaves with a clear action agenda that builds on the knowledge gained from research and moves the company forward.

Use Visual Maps to Convey Creative Insights

To help provide a fresh perspective on the consumer, make your presentation of insights as interesting and individualized as possible.

Some of the most useful briefings condense a great deal of information into a simple visual presentation that has impact through the use of diagrams or maps.

If your major insights come from a quantitative **perceptual mapping** study, you will have one or two maps of plotted data that will sum up huge amounts of information in a simple visual diagram. But even if you don't have quantitative data to generate a statistical diagram, you can use perceptual mapping techniques to convey your findings.

A recent qualitative study of watches found that consumers tend to categorize watch brands on the basis of a few interrelated characteristics. The first cut is between watches made by "watch companies" and those offered by clothing or accessory designers who also market clothing and other items and whose brands make a lifestyle statement, rather than convey particular characteristics of the watches. Designer watches are considered high style and trendy, while watches made by companies known only for their watches have a classic, timeless design that does not change from season to season.

In addition to the watchmaker's primary product focus, price, brand reputation, and availability combine to give some brands high status and others low or no status. High-status "watch company" brands convey imagery that says the wearer is knowledgeable about watches and has classic good taste. High-status "designer" brands relate more to the wearer's wealth and the lifestyle statement associated with each individual designer. Lower-status, lower-cost "designer" brands are semi-disposable fashion accessories chosen to match an outfit and are changed frequently, from day-to-day and season-to-season. Lower-cost "watch company" brands are more utilitarian, worn for functionality by people who look for a combination of conservative, classic style and good value.

In the research report documenting this study, findings relating to brand perceptions, consumer needs, and category opportunities were presented in great detail over many text-heavy pages. However, for presentation to the marketing team, the entire structure of the market, including brand perceptions, primary consumer motivations and potential new opportunities, was summarized in one page. The map shown in Figure 11.1 became the basis for discussing how to position and market a new entry into the category.

FIGURE 11.1

U.S. Wristwatch Perceptual Mapping

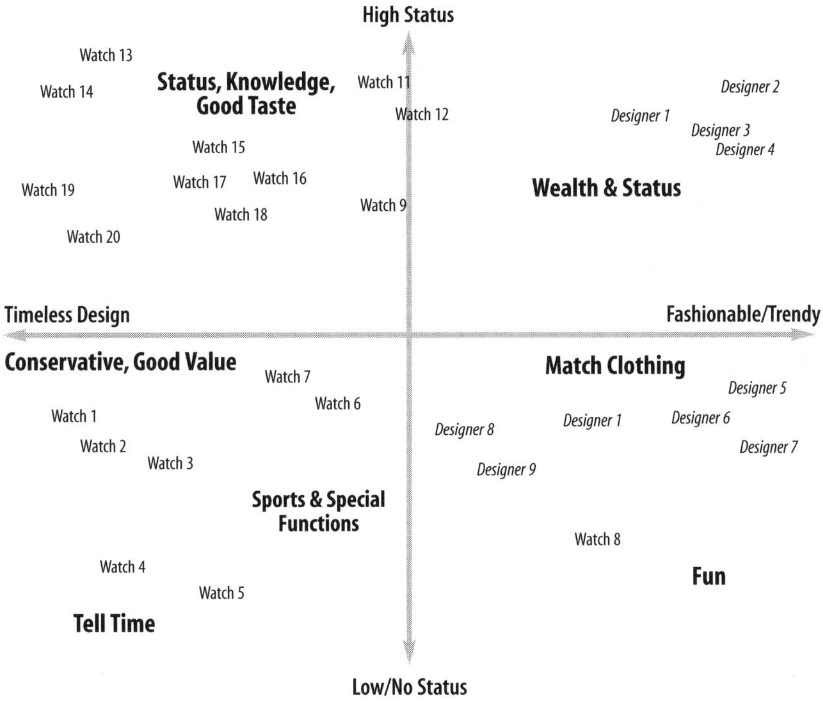

High Status

Watch 13

Watch 14   **Status, Knowledge, Good Taste**   Watch 11   Designer 2

Watch 12   Designer 1   Designer 3
Designer 4

Watch 15

Watch 19   Watch 17   Watch 16   **Wealth & Status**

Watch 18   Watch 9

Watch 20

Timeless Design   **Fashionable/Trendy**

Conservative, Good Value   Watch 7   **Match Clothing**

Designer 5

Watch 6

Watch 1   Designer 1   Designer 6

Designer 8

Watch 2   Designer 7

Watch 3   Designer 9

Sports & Special Functions

Watch 8

Watch 4   **Fun**

Watch 5

Tell Time

Low/No Status

To create this kind of map, you must have a good idea of category structure, including the criteria consumers use to differentiate one brand from another, and which brands are seen as similar to each other on each dimension. Many of the techniques described in Chapter 10 will produce this kind of information. Working with the raw data, you must identify the key factors and relationships that make the category structure meaningful to your problem, and make a diagram that shows their effect. When you work hard to find a way to convey masses of data in the simplest and most meaningful way possible, you are likely to find the insight that leads your team to a new level of understanding.

A **"leaky hose" analysis** uses metaphor to illustrate user drop-off or other situations where many elements begin a process and some fall off or drop out along the way, like water leaking out of a hose. If your marketing problem calls for an understanding of "trier-rejecters," or you want to understand a declining market share, the leaky hose may be a useful presentation technique that can sum up a great deal of information in a single memorable graphic.

FIGURE 11.2

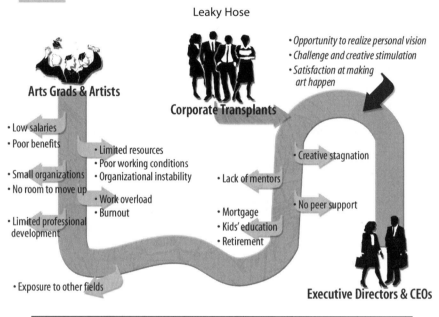

Leaky Hose

I used the leaky hose approach in 2003 to summarize results of a comprehensive study of leadership succession in arts organizations sponsored by the Illinois Arts Alliance and funded by the Chicago Community Trust. The research included interviews with present and former leaders of arts organizations, funders, board members and lower-level employees who aspire to leadership positions. Results of the whole project were reported in a number of ways, including books and a Leadership Succession Toolkit made available to arts organizations about to undergo a change in management.

To summarize findings of one aspect of the research, the Leaky Hose condensed a large quantity of data into one chart showing the typical arts management career path from the entry level to a top leadership post, and the many conditions and circumstances that cause people to leave the profession along the way.

A **mind map** or **concept map** can also be a powerful presentation tool that presents many related ideas in a single visual. It's an especially effective way to summarize the key findings from a study of consumer attitudes and motivations, since there can be complex relationships between attitudes that are not always easy to explain in words. Using a mind map, the arrangement of ideas and the direction of the lines you use to connect them graphically convey these relationships while keeping your analysis visual and memorable. There are several software programs that allow you to prepare complex mind maps quickly and easily. Some even let you use graphics, variations in colors and other devices to make your mind map meaningful.

For an example of a mind map presentation using only words, see Figure 11.3, which diagrams teenage attitudes toward driving based on what was learned in a series of focus group discussions with new drivers.

FIGURE 11.3

Mind Map

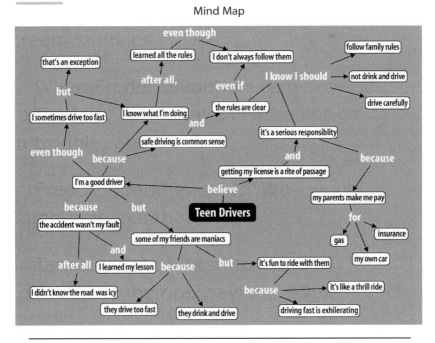

Turn Your Target Audience Profile into a Living, Breathing Consumer

Who is your target consumer? Can you identify your customers as individuals, or are you limited to a statistical profile that defines the most likely traits that describe your buyers? Most marketers are limited to working with profiles of their "typical" consumer, but there's no reason to make a presentation of these key traits dull, boring or confusing to your team. Breathing life into the portrait of your target consumer makes it easier for those who develop marketing programs to find creative ways to reach the prime audience.

One way to turn statistics into reality is to write a **target consumer biography** that gives your audience profile a personality and a life. If you've done the kind of research described in Chapter 8 to help you understand your target consumer's life and lifestyle, you should be able to summarize what you've learned in a one or two page description of a real person who epitomizes the profile you've developed. In this biography, give your consumer a name, an age, a place to live, an occupation, and a set of relatives and friends that fits the profile. Write what you know about her background, including educational level, ethnic identity or other characteristics. Use your analysis of lifestyle and values information to illustrate how your consumer thinks and feels about your product category: why she uses the product, what need it fulfills, what personal values it touches, and what makes her choose your brand or a competitor's. If it's relevant, include something about when and where she shops and how she uses the product, what her family thinks and feels, and what might make her become a heavier user, become more loyal, or stop buying your brand. Tell a story that links your consumer and your product, based on facts and rounded out with your intuition and insights.

Figure 11.4, "Karen Maxwell, Occasional Theater-Goer" is an example of a target consumer biography developed from several research studies profiling arts audiences in Chicago. In these studies, Chicago-area residents were asked about attendance at performing arts programs and visits to cultural institutions, as well as their

FIGURE 11.4

"Karen Maxwell, Occasional Theater-Goer"

KAREN MAXWELL, 43, lives in Oak Park, Illinois, where she also works as a part-time teacher's aide in a local elementary school. Karen and her husband Mike have three children—Jessica, 15, Amanda, 13, and Christopher, 8. They moved to Oak Park from Chicago when the girls were in pre-school. At first they lived in a condo near the El, so Mike could easily commute to his job as a consulting engineer in downtown Chicago. When Christopher came along, they sold the condo and bought a big old house that Karen has enjoyed renovating and decorating ever since.

Karen is a busy working mom who, now that the kids are getting older, feels it's important to make opportunities for the family to spend time together. She goes to all the school events and sports games that her children participate in, but sometimes, she likes to take them out of their everyday world, by involving them in the arts. Karen grew up going to museums, concerts, and the theater with her parents, and those outings represent some of her best memories of childhood. That's one reason she works hard to get her family involved in some of these same activities.

A few weekends a year, Karen and Mike take the whole family to one of Chicago's major museums, an outing that gives everyone a chance to have fun and at the same time, learn something new. In the summer, they attend art fairs and neighborhood festivals, which also gives the family a chance to learn about new cultures and have new experiences together.

Karen and her husband rarely attend theater as a couple. There's so little time, and Mike doesn't really enjoy the experience as much as she does. She wishes he would go more, but because he prefers other forms of entertainment, she relies on other family and her circle of friends for theater-going companionship. She sometimes takes Jessica and Amanda to smaller theaters in the city and suburbs to see new or unusual plays, and occasionally accepts an invitation to one of the better-known regional theaters downtown from a friend who has season tickets. Once a year or so, Karen and the girls take in a matinee performance downtown with Karen's sister and mother, an event they plan for weeks in advance. The girls enjoy picking out which show to see, deciding on where to go for lunch before the performance, and finding exactly the right thing to wear. Karen likes this outing because she feels it's a chance for her daughters to share a meaningful experience with their aunt and grandmother, while at the same time, getting exposure to a form of entertainment she wants them to appreciate.

She plans to start taking Christopher on theatre outings this year, although she's afraid it will be more difficult to find plays he'll want to see. She's glad that a couple of excellent new children's theater companies have sprung up recently, and she's keeping close watch on their schedules to find something that might appeal to her son. In the meantime, she enjoys her two or three times a year outings, and looks forward to a time when she has the time, energy, and disposable income to go as often as she'd like.

values, interests, attitudes, and leisure-time behavior and what they expect from their arts experiences. Combining these findings made it possible to create a vivid picture of a typical audience member's interests, concerns and motivations.

Remember That a Picture Is Worth a Thousand Words

Another way to make your consumer come alive is to visually depict as many aspects of his or her personality and lifestyle as you can. If you've done any in-home observations, take photos of your respondents' homes and present a **neighborhood montage** of these images to convey a sense of their lifestyles and personalities.

If your research included having consumers make collages or drawings, you can pick out the most interesting ones to illustrate the results of these exercises. However, even if your research doesn't include collage making, your presentation can. Just take what you know about your target consumer, based on all the research you've conducted, and make your own **consumer lifestyle collage** to show what he or she is all about. Use literal and symbolic cues. If he's a sports fan, you'll want sports-related images, but think about whether he participates in his favorite sports or is just a passive spectator. For the former, make sure your collage shows plenty of action and uses vibrant colors that convey the feeling of an exciting game. For the latter, you might want to use more subdued tones, more sedate images, and a TV screen or two. Add some cues as to your typical target consumer's lifestage, occupation, and educational achievement. Include some references to his interests, hobbies, and the primary needs your product can fulfill. If you couple your imagination with the knowledge you've gained from target audience research, your collage will be a memorable depiction of a living, breathing human being your whole team will recognize.

Another way to use pictures is to include **video clips** from focus groups and individual interviews in your presentations. Usually, it's best not to overload your results with video clips. A written quote accompanied by a good close-up photo of the person speaking is often a quicker and more effective method of capturing consumer language and mood. However, there are times when short passages from an interview or a focus group convey your insight more effectively than any other method. Be prepared for such moments by planning ahead. Instead of using the standard fixed-position video cameras most facilities use to record focus groups, ask for a human video operator who can focus in on individual speakers. During an interview, make notes of the time when a respondent says something that may be especially quotable. Include only a few of the very best clips in your presentation, or you'll be bogged down in an endless replay of the original interviews. For more depth, put longer clips on a DVD or a video file accessible on your company Intranet, so team members can spend as much time as they like getting their own immersion in the consumer.

Appendix A

Ten Exercises for Developing Your Personal Insights Capabilities

IF YOU'VE READ THIS FAR, you should have a good idea of what insights are all about, how consumer insights can make a contribution to your business, and even how to go about a search for the information that will lead to insights. But even if you study the theories, use the techniques and take great pains to present your results creatively, there's still no guarantee that you'll come up with great insights. Finding the relevant but unexpected piece of information that leads to a breakthrough idea takes patience. Recognizing the hidden gem takes practice. To build your insight-producing muscles, try this ten-part insights workout.

1. **Identify a trend or fad.** Not something you read, or something you hear about on TV. Not something someone else says is happening. Look around for signs of something new that's ready to become the next big thing.

   Start by observing what's around you. Take frequent walks in areas where there are lots of people—a busy city street, a shopping mall, or anywhere else where people gather. Look at everyone you see. What do you notice about how they are dressed? What they are doing? What they are talking about? Do the same thing riding public transportation, or spend some time in an airport, a busy diner or a coffee house. What are people doing to pass the time? If you see someone reading, try to figure out what the book or article is about. If they are listening to music or playing video games, notice the device they are using, and how they interact with it. If they are talking on their cell phones, feel free to eavesdrop. Listen for interesting expressions, new slang you haven't heard before, or comments about current events or famous people. Pay special attention to teenagers. They are particularly likely to adopt new or different ways of dressing and talking that the rest of us will soon pick up.

Once you've noticed something new, look for other instances of the same or similar behavior. Think about whether what you've observed is related in any way to popular culture. Have you seen something similar on TV, or in a movie? Has the subject been featured in a magazine? Use a search engine to see what's on the Internet. Pay attention for signs of your new trend if you have the chance to observe any focus groups, or read polling data. Keep looking for connections or relationships in whatever situations you encounter.

Once you've accumulated a few instances of what seems like a new phenomenon, try to formulate a theory that explains what's behind its emergence. A few years ago, for instance, cosmetic surgery suddenly seemed to move to the forefront of everyone's attention. Instead of denying they'd had a procedure, people started bragging about the work they'd had done, or were planning to have done. Magazines started touting plastic surgery for men. Several television shows took up the topic, from the fictional *Nip/Tuck* to the all-too-real *Extreme Makeover*. Political candidates and their wives admitted to using a little Botox. Cosmetic surgery went from being a secret luxury of the rich and vain to something almost anyone could imagine doing, and something many ordinary people actually did.

What caused the emergence of cosmetic surgery from an elite to a mass activity? There were several factors at work, but one important influence was the aging of the Baby Boom generation. As more Boomers passed fifty and saw sixty rapidly approaching, cosmetic surgery became more generally acceptable. The basic demographic trend of aging was combined with a booming economy in the late 1990s that gave more people the income they needed to pay for discretionary cosmetic procedures. New medical techniques also played a role. No longer was there a choice between doing nothing or undergoing major surgery with several weeks of recovery. A quick Botox injection or a little liposuction could be done in an afternoon, with the patient out dancing that same night and back at work the next day.

Look for similar explanations for the phenomenon you observe. When you identify possible causes, you'll be in a better position to decide whether what you're seeing is a trend or a fad. You'll also be able to assess what, if any, influence it will have on your business.

As a conclusion to your practice exercise, write a paragraph or two on the trend you have identified. Put it away for a few months, and then look again to see how accurate your assessment was. In the meantime, keep looking around. The next big thing is right around the corner.

2. **Spend time experiencing someone else's life** to get some practice in changing your point of view. Take what you know about your target customers and try to incorporate their experiences into your own life. Shop for groceries on their weekly budget. Do the things they do for fun, whether it's attending a NASCAR race or going to the opera. Eat foods they particularly like, especially if your target group has a different regional or ethnic background from your own. Watch their favorite television shows. Eat in their favorite restaurants. If they have young children and you don't, find a willing family and do some babysitting, or take a niece or nephew to the zoo for an afternoon. If you're marketing to teens, make friends with a local high school principal and offer to chaperone a school dance, or start going to the school's sporting events. Get out of your own life and try on aspects of someone else's.

3. **Make a target consumer your imaginary friend.** Based on everything you know about your target audience, visualize a real person. Give him a name and a life. Treat her the way a child treats

an imaginary friend. Talk together—in private, unless you like getting odd looks from passing strangers. Ask questions. Listen to what your friend has to say. Let your imagination take over and you'll be surprised at how much your imaginary friend will reveal.

4. **Watch reality TV for insights, not entertainment.** Although the "reality" that gets on the air may not always be the whole truth, you can learn by watching. Pay attention to shows that give you a look at how people live their lives. Programs like *Supernanny* or *Wife Swap* will get you into the homes of real families, and can reveal interesting family dynamics. Makeover shows can give you a better understanding of consumer taste in home decorating and personal style. Transformational shows like *The Biggest Loser* or *Beauty and the Geek* can show how different people address specific problems in their lives. As you watch these shows, think about what the participants say and do, what's important to them, and how they might relate to your brand or how they might use your product.

5. **Take an acting class.** The essence of method acting is "becoming" the character you are trying to portray. Actors learn to draw on their own experiences to empathize with the emotions and sensations of their characters, in order to fit naturally into their roles. Learning the techniques actors use to get into the head of their characters will help you get into the heads of consumers in the same way.

6. **Read newspapers and general interest magazines regularly.** In the age of targeted media, these publications are almost the only places where you can stumble across new things you have not previously identified as of interest to you. Unlike television news, print media are able to include all sorts of stories, from in-depth analysis of foreign affairs to light features on new forms of recreation. Read a good newspaper every day for three months, and you'll be amazed at how many things you know about that others around you may have missed.

7. **Watch or listen to foreign news broadcasts.** It's another way to practice seeing things from a different perspective. Most cable and satellite systems, and many public television and radio stations, carry daily news programs from the BBC and may also include programs from other countries, in English or other languages. My own cable system has at various times offered news from Ireland, The United Kingdom, Italy, Poland, France, Russia, and The Philippines, along with Spanish-language U.S. news on several channels. Even if you don't speak the language, tune in to these programs when a big news story breaks. You'll get a valuable lesson in seeing things from a different point of view.

8. **Mine an old research study for new insights.** Pull something off the shelf and see if you can find a new bit of information that was missed or ignored in the original analysis. Skip past the summary and conclusions and dig into the actual findings. Ask new questions. Let yourself wonder what caused or motivated the reported behaviors. Think about the implications of the attitudes that are documented. Then apply your new insights to the old problem the study was designed to address. If someone had noticed what you are now seeing, would they have made a different decision? Taken different actions? Ended up with a different result? Go a little further, and think about what your new insight means for the business issues you are dealing with today. Try applying your findings to a current problem or issue. Remember that a new question does not necessarily require a new study. Building on what you already know is an important principle of consumer insights.

9. **Take a class or learn a new skill.** Choose something that seems to be completely unrelated to your work. It will help you step away and let your mind relax. It will also generate some new energy and give you an additional tool to use in your quest for insights.

10. **Pay attention to what people are laughing at.** Humor is an important reflection of what people care about, what concerns them, and what they want to change. So pay attention to comedy. It can

help reveal a whole host of insights. Stay up for the monologue from Leno or Letterman, watch Comedy Central, visit a comedy club or notice what gets the most laughs on *Saturday Night Live*. Pay attention to the jokes people tell in casual conversation. Develop your own sense of humor, and learn to appreciate the humor of others. It will keep you smiling, and it might also make you a little more insightful.

Appendix B

Ten Steps for Making Consumer Insights Part of Your Organization

IF YOU'RE A CEO, CMO or other high-level executive who believes in consumer insights, there are specific steps you can take to make your organization more insights-friendly. If you're not at that level, start doing what you can to make these changes. As your new insights demonstrate their worth, you'll see the organization become more willing to adopt the changes that will make your approach even more effective.

To create an organizational culture in which consumer insights drive business success, take these ten steps.

1. **Make a long-term commitment to the insights approach.** If your organization has a long history of inward focus, or a marketing research department that is comfortable with its traditional role, change will not happen quickly. You can start slowly, introducing consumer-insights tools and techniques and allocating limited resources for new investigative endeavors, but you must be willing to stick with it until the approach becomes second nature.

2. **Put responsibility for consumer insights in the hands of the right person.** The leader of your consumer insights effort needs to have a combination of research skills, business savvy, and creativity. He or she also needs a strong personal commitment to the idea. You can't impose consumer insights on a reluctant marketing research director or marketing officer. You need a leader who can be an advocate within the organization—someone with a strong base of

experience and credibility who can be a champion for insights at all levels of the company.

3. **Be clear about what you consider an insight.** Don't be willing to accept surface-level findings or interpretations and call them insights. If an insight seems generic or obvious, it probably won't be too helpful. Push to get deeper below the surface, to identify the needs, emotions and motivations that really matter. One company asks insight-seekers to look for messages that represent the highest compliment they could possibly give the target consumer. Others define the key insight as the connection between what the consumer wants and what the brand can uniquely offer. Your definition might incorporate ideas such as reinforcing loyalty, touching an emotional cord, or tapping into the consumer's core values. However you express it, make sure everyone involved in the search for insights can recognize one when they find it.

4. **Define a specific role for consumer insights** in your organization's strategic planning process. Start asking for the "key insight" behind any marketing recommendation. Require brand managers and other program planners to reference information about consumers in their plans, and to explain the implications of their consumer understanding in support of their recommendations.

5. **Keep moving forward, even if insights are slow in coming.** Don't allow your business to be crippled by analysis paralysis in the quest for the perfect insight. Sometimes, it takes moving forward with a less than perfect idea to really learn. Even when no great insights emerge, make decisions based on the best information you have, and keep trying to improve as you go along.

6. **Make consumer insights part of the corporate conversation.** Use the language of insights when you talk about how your company makes decisions. Find ways to incorporate consumer-consciousness into the work of every department. Publicize examples of how uncovering a key insight led to a better marketing program or more successful new product. Let people know that pushing for better, deeper, richer insights pays off in more success.

7. **Insist on insights-based new product development.** Insights-driven new product development is the exact opposite of "if we build it, they will come" thinking. It's true that consumers often don't realize they want or need a new product until it's actually on the market, but new products are rarely successful if they fail to address a fundamental consumer need, desire, or complaint. Search for insights into territory ripe for new ideas or improved performance, and concentrate your company's technological expertise on meeting those needs.

8. **Build a body of consumer knowledge, one project at a time.** Stop wasting time on "disposable" research studies that shed light on one small issue and never come off the library shelf again. Concentrate time and resources on projects that build a body of knowledge. Keep a running list of issues to investigate, and as new areas of interest emerge, start each new effort with an analysis of what you already know. Look for trends in your own data. Make the most of all the information you have.

9. **Be willing to experiment.** Try new approaches to information gathering and analysis. Give your consumer insights group some latitude to be creative. Put some money in the budget for developing new techniques. Make sure they have the freedom to fail, even as you set high expectations for success.

10. **Spread consumer insights beyond marketing.** Let insights specialists get involved in all aspects of the business. Encourage them to consult with any department that needs their help, and share their fundamental understanding of the consumer with everyone who might benefit. When departments who never thought they could benefit from marketing research start talking about decisions based on consumer insights, you'll know you're making progress. When those decisions lead to business breakthroughs, you'll know you have succeeded.

Suggested Reading

Consumer insights can come from anywhere and everywhere. Reading widely is one way to stimulate thinking and build your capacity for developing creative ways of looking at the world. This list includes just a sampling of the books I've used over the years to build insight and understanding.

Advertising and Account Planning

Dru, Jean-Marie. *Disruption: Overturning Conventions and Shaking Up the Marketplace*. Adweek Books, John Wiley & Sons, Inc., New York, 1996.

Fortini-Campbell, Lisa. *Hitting the Sweet Spot: How Consumer Insights Can Inspire Better Marketing and Advertising*. The Copy Workshop, Chicago IL, 2001.

Rothenberg, Randall. *Where the Suckers Moon: An Advertising Story*. Alfred A. Knopf, New York, 1994.

Steel, Jon. *Truth, Lies & Advertising: The Art of Account Planning*. Adweek Books, John Wiley & Sons, Inc., New York, 1998.

Zyman, Sergio. *The End of Marketing As We Know It*. Harper Business, A Division of Harper Collins, New York, 1999, 2000.

Zyman, Sergio. *The End of Advertising As We Know It*. John Wiley & Sons, Inc., Hoboken, NJ, 2002.

Consumer Behavior

Cialdini, Robert B. *Influence: The Psychology of Persuasion*. Quill William Morris, New York, 1984, 1991.

Gladwell, Malcolm. *Blink: The Power of Thinking Without Thinking*. Little Brown and Company, Time Warner Book Group, New York, 2005.

Gladwell, Malcolm. *The Tipping Point: How Little Things Can Make A Big Difference*. Little, Brown and Company, Time Warner Book Group, New York, 2000, 2002.

Johansson, Franz. *The Medici Effect: Breakthrough Insights at the Intersection of Ideas, Concepts and Culture*. Harvard Business School Press, Boston, MA, 2004.

Schwartz, Barry. *The Paradox of Choice: Why More is Less*. Harper Collins Publishers, Inc., New York, 2004.

Strauss, Willam and Howe, Neil. *The Fourth Turning: An American Prophecy*. Broadway Books, A Division of Doubleday, New York, 1997.

Strauss, William and Howe, Neil. *Generations: The History of America's Future 1584 to 2069*. William Morrow and Company, New York, 1991.

Wind, Yoram (Jerry) and Crook, Colin, with Gunther, Robert. *The Power of Impossible Thinking*. Wharton School Publishing, Upper Saddle River, NJ, 2005.

Zaltman, Gerald. *How Customers Think: Essential Insights Into the Mind of the Market*. Harvard Business School Press, Boston, MA, 2003.

Consumer Segments and Lifestyles

Brooks, David. *Bobos in Paradise: The New Upper Class and How They Got There*. A Touchstone Book, Simon & Schuster, New York, 2000.

Ehrenreich, Barbara. *Nickel and Dimed: On (Not) Getting By in America*. Henry Holt & Company, New York, 2001.

Florida, Richard. *The Rise of the Creative Class*. Basic Books, A Member of the Perseus Book Group, New York, 2002.

Keller, Ed and Berry, Jon. *The Influentials*. The Free Press, A Division of Simon & Schuster, New York, 2003.

Miller, Pepper and Kemp, Herb. *What's Black About It? Insights to Increase Your Share of a Changing African-American Market.* Paramount Market Publishing, Inc., Ithaca, NY, 2005.

Marketing Research Tools and Techniques

Bystedt, Jean; Lynn, Siri, & Potts, Deborah. *Moderating to the MAX!* Paramount Market Publishing, Inc., Ithaca, NY, 2003.

Langer, Judith. *The Mirrored Window: Focus Groups from a Moderator's Point of View.* Paramount Market Publishing, Inc., Ithaca, NY, 2001.

Mariampolski, Hy. *Ethnography for Marketers: A Guide to Consumer Immersion.* Sage Publications, Thousand Oaks, CA, 2006.

Orme, Bryan K. *Getting Started with Conjoint Analysis: Strategies for Product Design and Pricing Research.* Research Publications LLC, Madison, WI, 2005.

Qualitative Research Consultants Association. *QRCA Views.* Published quarterly by Leading Edge Communications.

Quirk's Marketing Research Review, Published 11 times a year by Quirk's Publishing, Eagan, MN.

Index

About the Author

Dona Vitale has been an independent qualitative research consultant since 1987 when she established Strategic Focus, Inc. in Chicago. Before striking out on her own, Ms. Vitale worked at Foote, Cone & Belding Advertising as Vice President/Associate Research Director, and in various positions in direct and database marketing. At FCB, she worked with clients including Kraft Foods, S.C. Johnson, The Adolph Coors Company and Sunkist Orange Soda, developing new research techniques and new methods of analysis to meet each client's needs.

Since becoming a qualitative research consultant, Ms. Vitale has conducted more than 2,000 focus group and individual interviews, observational research, and ethnography projects for consumer products companies as well as a diverse group of cultural institutions, government agencies, and arts organizations.

Ms. Vitale has taught marketing research classes in the University of Chicago's Graham School of Continuing Studies Integrated Marketing program since 1999, and first developed a course in consumer insights in 2004. She also teaches workshops in Target Audience Segmentation, Trendwatching, and Conducting Audience Research in the National Arts Marketing Program of the Arts and Business Council of Friends of the Arts. She has made presentations on research issues at various meetings of the Advertising Research Foundation, The

American Marketing Association, the Arts and Business Council, the Association for Commuter Transportation and the Transportation Research Board.

On the personal side, she travels extensively for pleasure when not traveling for business. She is an enthusiastic amateur photographer, and spends much time at home restoring and decorating a 90-year-old house on Chicago's North Side.

Ms. Vitale holds a MBA degree (with honors) from the Northwestern University Kellogg Graduate School of Management, with a specialty in Marketing. She is also an honors graduate of Michigan State University College of Communication Arts, with a major in Advertising and a minor in Social Psychology (attitude formation and change).